PRAISE FOR *BETTER & BETTER*

"Bob Stiller was an early mover in using the tools of business to make change. He has written a vital and compelling account of the Green Mountain principles and practices that helped the world embrace better ways of doing business and understand who makes our coffee possible. A must read for all who care."
—**Jacqueline Novogratz**, founder and CEO of Acumen

"*Better & Better* tells the incredible story of how Bob Stiller pioneered socially conscious business practices from ESOPs to mindfulness to Fair Trade. Bob's visionary leadership helped build the Fair Trade movement in the US, raising standards for sustainability in the coffee industry and improving the lives of millions of coffee farmers and their families."
—**Paul Rice**, founder and CEO of Fair Trade USA

"Bob Stiller embodies what it means to get things done and take an enterprise from zero to a billion with incredible integrity and care. This is a necessary manual for anyone who wants to understand how success derives from our core values."
—**David Allen**, international bestselling author of
Getting Things Done

"The epic rise of Green Mountain is one of the most inspiring business stories of our century. In this gem of a book, Bob Stiller offers six powerful principles for unlocking human potential and making business a force for good in the world."
—**David L. Cooperrider**, author of *The Business of Building a Better World* and *Appreciative Inquiry: A Positive Revolution in Change*

"*Better & Better* is rich with insightful observations, useful advice, and engaging storytelling. Bob Stiller saw Green Mountain as more than just a balance sheet. It was a partnership—with his employees, his community, and the world."

—**Lorna Davis**, former CEO of Danone North America

"Bob Stiller did more than just make exceptional coffee and build a thriving company. He showed a passionate desire to serve people and the planet, engaging workers at every point in the supply chain and creating a caring and happy organizational culture we can all embrace."

—**Roberta Baskin**, award-winning journalist

"Before Green Mountain Coffee Roasters, coffee was another cheap commodity. Bob Stiller's once-small Vermont company created a booming market for more expensive, high-quality, ethically-sourced coffee. He set a new standard for the industry by rewarding employees for thinking beyond convention about what a business could be."

—**Dan Cox**, president of Coffee Enterprises, SCAA Lifetime
   Achievement recipient

"Bob Stiller didn't invent single serve coffee, but he clearly saw opportunity that others were ignoring. *Better & Better* relates how he added layers of holistic management and engagement to create opportunity for his people to thrive as the company prospered. The book reveals an enterprise becoming more successful as shared values inspired creativity and commitment."

—**Jerry Baldwin**, former owner/CEO of Peet's Coffee,
   cofounder/CEO of Starbucks

"Tucked inside this insightful blueprint is how Bob Stiller's leadership inspired one of the most effective social change movements in recent memory, guided by the same principles he honed throughout his career in business. Bob's experience proves that doing the right thing, for our people and our planet, is the surest path to success, no matter where you choose to make your impact."

—**Aly Richards**, CEO of *Let's Grow Kids*

Better & Better

Better&
Better

Creating a Culture of Purpose,
Excellence, and Transformative
Human Engagement

BOB STILLER

Mc
Graw
Hill

1 2 3 4 5 LBC 28 27 26 25 24

ISBN   978-1-265-46084-6
MHID   1-265-46084-1

e-ISBN   978-1-265-46113-3
e-MHID   1-265-46113-9

This publication is designed to provide accurate and authoritative information in regard to the subject matter covered. It is sold with the understanding that neither the author nor the publisher is engaged in rendering legal, accounting, securities trading, or other professional services. If legal advice or other expert assistance is required, the services of a competent professional person should be sought.
—*From a Declaration of Principles Jointly Adopted by a Committee of the American Bar Association and a Committee of Publishers and Associations*

McGraw Hill books are available at special quantity discounts to use as premiums and sales promotions or for use in corporate training programs. To contact a representative, please visit the Contact Us pages at www.mhprofessional.com.

McGraw Hill is committed to making our products accessible to all learners. To learn more about the available support and accommodations we offer, please contact us at accessibility@mheducation.com. We also participate in the Access Text Network (www.accesstext.org), and ATN members may submit requests through ATN.

*To Christine and our children Julie, David,
and Christian, in appreciation of
your love, support, and inspiration*

CONTENTS

INTRODUCTION

I am writing this book with the benefit of three decades' perspective leading a company, reflecting on what made us so successful, how we engaged our employees and stakeholders with purpose and made the world a better place. Founding and growing Keurig Green Mountain was one of the most exciting eras of my life. Years ago, I thought about writing a book to tell our story and pay tribute to the employees and stakeholders who came together around a higher purpose and executed with excellence in pursuing our mission. But I wondered what difference it could really make.

Friends, family members, and former colleagues eventually convinced me that telling the story of how we changed the coffee industry—leading on Fair Trade and social responsibility, shifting from drip coffee to single-serve machines, and more—would be interesting for some. And the story of how we cultivated a high-engagement culture—becoming one of just four billion-dollar coffee companies in the United States—could be helpful for many more.

While I always saw running Green Mountain as an intuitive matter of "doing the right thing," I've come to see that the way we did things was really quite rare and special. We were charting our own course in many ways, but many of the elements that created our work culture have since been researched, their effectiveness confirmed. Still, many companies have been slow to embrace them.

In a changing world of work, where employers are challenged to provide not just a livelihood, but meaningful opportunities for engagement and growth, I believe that there is a benefit in sharing what we accomplished, and more important, how we did it. I've undertaken the writing of this book to share our journey and those lessons.

This book will tell how a highly engaged community of ordinary people transformed a tiny coffee roaster in a Vermont ski town into a multibillion-dollar publicly traded company that not only changed the way Americans consume coffee, but defined and validated a new and better way of doing business. At Green Mountain Coffee, we believed that our financial fate was closely linked to the happiness and success of our employees and all the stakeholders of our company. Our philosophy was that personal development, higher purpose, and the pursuit of profit were all inextricably intertwined. We built our business on the power of transformative human engagement.

This way of seeing business is more relevant today than ever before. In an age of loneliness and disconnection, business students, young entrepreneurs, and corporate executives—and arguably an entire generation—are looking for organizations to lead with purpose and compassion. I hope I can instill in you my unwavering belief that leading with purpose, mindfulness, and the intentional engagement of employees and stakeholders creates extraordinary motivation, creativity, and results for everyone.

Better & Better will offer an unprecedented insider's view into the challenges, hard work, big decisions, and learnings of my 30-plus years running Green Mountain Coffee and leading the way on sustainability, corporate social responsibility, and progressive workplace benefits. It will also offer an experience-based guide to the mindset, policies, and practices required to build an intentional business that outperforms because it values and engages all the organization's stakeholders. This Introduction will set forth what I call the Better and Better Blueprint, a set of seven key strategic principles and priorities that I believe capture the essence of what made Green Mountain coffee so successful. I did not have this blueprint while I served as CEO, although I wish I had. Rather, I learned along the way, intuitively seeking a path—and studying what worked. The resulting blueprint is a distillation of that hard-earned wisdom.

Our story shows that meteoric growth is not incompatible with working to make the world a better place. In fact, they go hand in hand. Between 1999 and 2009, Green Mountain shares rose 7,895 percent, and we were the top-performing Nasdaq stock for the decade. If you had invested $13,000 in Green Mountain stock in 1999, it would have been worth more than a million dollars in 2009, if you held on to it.[1] (Luckily, many of our employees did, becoming millionaires through our employee stock ownership program.)

The chances of building a billion-dollar business are 0.00006 percent.[2] We not only achieved that, but did so in a way that modeled the power of business to be a positive agent of change. In 2005, Green Mountain was the first company in the coffee industry to support the United Nation's Global Reporting Initiative, which developed globally accepted sustainability reporting guidelines.[3] Well before CSR (corporate social responsibility) or ESG (environmental, social, and governance) practices were on the radar of almost any major business, we were giving 5 percent of our pretax profits to support sustainable coffee projects, coffee-growing communities, and social causes worldwide. At our peak, in 2012, we gave nearly $19 million annually through these programs—a far greater amount, percentage-wise, than other companies. We were one of the pioneers in the Fair Trade movement and became the world's largest buyer of organic and Fair Trade–certified coffee in the world. And by stimulating greater demand for Fair Trade–certified coffee, we helped shift the coffee industry away from a focus on price—the cost to consumers—to a focus on shared value creation for all stakeholders.

Supporting coffee-growing communities and leading on Fair Trade and organic coffee certification—these defining elements of Green Mountain's culture reflected the values of our employees. And as we saw the impact that our efforts were having—connecting our remarkable team in Vermont to improvements in the lives of coffee farming communities that many of us got to know personally—it became a source of motivation more powerful than money. Our coffee-growing partners were equally motivated by seeing how much we cared about and appreciated their work. Our shared mission enabled us to press forward even in the toughest times, and it ultimately drove exponential gains in our revenue and our impact. Our purpose statement, co-created with our employees, had a deep meaning to everyone: "We create the ultimate coffee experience in every life we touch from tree to cup—transforming the way the world understands business."

Doing business in a way that values all stakeholders isn't just the right thing to do; it's a more effective way of doing business. There is a growing body of research showing that socially and environmentally conscious companies outperform peers that neglect these values. Such compassionate brands resonate more with consumers—84 percent of consumers in the 2021 IBM Institute for Business Value survey, for example, said that sustainability was important to them in choosing a brand.[4] And according to a study of nearly 1,300 global companies by the Centre for Economics and Business Research/Moore Global, between 2019 and 2022, companies embracing ESG principles saw revenue growth more than twice that of companies that disregarded ESG considerations (9.7 percent versus 4.5 percent), and enjoyed higher revenues and greater access to finance.[5]

Why are these companies more successful? It isn't just that consumers and investors had a more positive perception of them. It's the fact that employees at these companies felt more engaged at work. They cared more.

The benefits of an engaged workforce are legion. In 2020, a Gallup meta-analysis of research across industries and countries found that high-engagement businesses enjoyed advantages over low-engagement peers that include 81 percent less absenteeism, 41 percent fewer quality defects, 10 percent greater consumer loyalty, and 23 percent higher profitability.[6]

The enthusiasm of our workforce was unequaled, and I believe it was a key ingredient in the secret sauce that enabled us to prosper where so many others failed. Yes, we developed a great product, marketed it well, and developed innovative ways for customers to enjoy it. But so did many of our competitors. The reason we succeeded against many bigger and more experienced players is that, collectively, we were simply more engaged and executed better than anyone else. We enjoyed an employee retention rate of 90 percent—and in our 2009 employee survey, 93 percent of employees said that Green Mountain was "a great place to work." Creating this sense of purpose, belonging, joy, and commitment to seeking positive change in your own life and for others—the collective sense that we were an organization where people could be their full selves while thriving together—is what these days I like to refer to as "transformative human engagement."

You may be asking yourself, "Just how did they create a culture of such transformative human engagement?" After all, this seems to be the holy grail for businesses in the post-COVID Great Resignation era, when "quiet quitting" is the norm. In Gallup's State of the Global Workplace 2023 Report, only 23 percent of workers globally say they are "engaged" at work, while 59 percent are "quiet quitting" (not engaged) and 18 percent are actively disengaged.[7] More than ever, there is an urgency to the challenge of keeping employees motivated and connected, of creating and maintaining an inspiring common culture.

The consistent and varied recognition and awards that Green Mountain received for sustainability and social programs motivated and inspired the organization. Current research shows that employees want that more than ever. In the 2021 IBM Institute for Business Value survey, roughly 70 percent of the potential workforce say they're more likely to apply for and accept a job with an organization they consider to be environmentally sustainable and socially responsible.[8]

In this new, highly competitive market for talent, a company needs to be more than just a place to work. Nearly nine in ten employees believe it is no longer acceptable for a company just to make money.[9] To be successful today, companies must unleash the creative energy and enthusiasm of their workforce, meeting their calls for sustainable and socially responsible business practices and progressive work environments. They need to be seen as places where people can make a difference, where their input matters, where they're fairly rewarded, and where they can grow. Places they feel good about. Places where they are fully engaged. *Places where they believe that everyone involved—across the entire enterprise—is consistently striving to do better and better.*

This is exactly what we cultivated at Green Mountain: a place where people were cared for, and cared. A place where people were asked to come together to learn and to grow—and they did. More than a simple chronology of our rise as a company—including the bumps and bruises we encountered along the way—this book will describe the puzzle pieces we put together that resulted in a whole that was greater than the sum of its parts.

While I may not have been following an explicit blueprint as I built Green Mountain, looking back, I recognize that we intentionally leveraged a variety of strategies that resulted in a level of human engagement and conscientiousness that can only be described as transformative. We engaged coffee farmers and their families; partners who financed the farmers; those who roasted the coffee, packaged the coffee, and sold the coffee; social entrepreneurs at non-profits such as Fair Trade USA; and of course all our employees and people across the communities in which we operated. This is what propelled our success.

The Better and Better Blueprint—summarized below—posits that by pursuing seven principles (in various combinations), we created a positive combustion of personal engagement far greater than any single approach could have achieved. Taken separately, none of these ideas are necessarily new. There is a litany of research that has validated the benefits of many Green Mountain initiatives: employee stock ownership plans, Appreciative Inquiry, meditation, open-book management, commitments to environmental sustainability, employee development programs, social responsibility initiatives, and more.

What was unique, however, was bringing together what to date had been treated as disparate approaches. These principles didn't work alone; rather, the innovative initiatives we pursued in my three decades running the business were informed by layering multiple principles on top of each other—like a chord instead of a single-note melody. (The principles are interrelated and can be undertaken in any order.) This multiplicative effect fueled the transformative engagement of all our company's stakeholders. I believe that this, in turn, drove our overall success. In summary, we worked to do the following:

1. **Sustain an opportunity mindset.** We cultivated awareness of the possibilities within everything (including people, products, and processes) and constantly worked to convert potential into tangible outcomes.
2. **Co-create excellence.** We continuously strove to improve together, enhancing individuals, products, processes, and systems and positively impacting lives both within and beyond the company.
3. **Pursue a higher purpose.** We held the unapologetic stance that business is, and must be, a powerful force for good in the world. Recognizing the power of doing good, we sought to inspire others to make a difference, too.
4. **Value all stakeholders.** We extended appreciation, respect, and compassion for the unique identities, attributes, and strengths of every stakeholder within and beyond the company (including the natural environment) from "tree to cup." We worked together for our mutual success.
5. **Cultivate mindfulness, learning, and well-being.** We encouraged meditation practices to support individuals' inner clarity, and we honored holistic well-being. We fostered awareness of how our choices and mindset shape the future.
6. **Seek high points of the past and future.** To leverage the universe of strengths throughout the organization, we consistently inquired into and celebrated what was best in our individual and collective past and collectively imagined a positive future.
7. **Share positive experiences.** We believed that offering frequent and direct experiences of our brand was key to winning hearts and engaging minds.

In the chapters that follow, I will share how Green Mountain employees both shaped and shared in the company's success—through stock purchase programs that created more than a few millionaires, and through progressive workplace benefits that were consistently recognized as best in class. Because of the opportunities we offered employees to grow through education and training programs, along with the exceptional benefits and stock ownership programs we instituted, we were the first company to be ranked number 1 for two consecutive years on the list of 100 Best Corporate Citizens by *CRO Magazine*.[10] More than our stock performance—or even the financial rewards we shared with both employees and partners—the best reflection of what we accomplished was the cohesive, bighearted community of stakeholders we created together.

My own leadership style is pragmatic, participative, and transformational, supported by a meditation practice that, in turn, inspired my commitment to embedding mindfulness and well-being in the culture of Green Mountain (see Chapter 5). My approach to business was also influenced by having grown up watching my father run a successful company that manufactured tubular heating elements (which I reflect further on in Chapter 1). It was he who instilled in me what was originally a three-part formula for business success: make the best-quality product, provide the best service, and take care of your employees. The importance of quality products and services was at the core of our continual pursuit of excellence, embodied by my mantra, "Better and better," which echoed throughout Green Mountain (see Chapter 2). What was perhaps unique about our approach to continuous improvement was making it an exercise in co-creation, intentionally engaging employees, customers, and all other stakeholders (see Chapter 3).

Many businesses today understand those first two variables in my father's formula but skimp on the third: taking care of employees. I have always been committed to providing training and development to improve the skills of my employees. Individual excellence drives organizational excellence. I was always concerned with making sure that people understood how they contributed to our business, how their work impacted the world, and how much I valued and needed their input—whether it was about a small operational improvement or a major strategic initiative. While I have since added a few more variables to my father's three-part formula, these three principles for success echo in the Better and Better Blueprint, as I will underscore throughout the book.

At Green Mountain Coffee, I encouraged a radically open culture. Through open-book management training in business principles, I engaged employees at all levels of the business in growing the company with me. And, crucially, by employing the philosophy and methods of Appreciative Inquiry—developed by Case Western University Weatherhead School of Management professors David Cooperrider and Suresh Srivastva—we invited employees, customers, and other stakeholders to join us in lively, collaborative "summits" to seek the high points of the past that could help drive future improvements (see Chapter 6). [11]

Green Mountain's culture came to encompass many partnerships outside the company, too—manifested in all our interactions with customers, suppliers, nongovernmental organizations, and other stakeholders around the world. In this book, I will show how the quality of these *external* interactions—mirroring the collaborative culture *inside* the company—came to define our brand in the marketplace, cementing our success. The importance of stakeholder engagement has been confirmed by research, including a study showing that from 2000 to 2020, stakeholder-focused companies saw their shares rise 100 percent higher than the S&P 500.[12]

Our list of "stakeholders" also included the natural environment—a radical notion at the time. After all, without coffee trees, we could not have anything to go from "tree to cup" with! This commitment to ensuring that both people and the planet were better off through our work became the heartbeat of Green Mountain's pursuit of a higher purpose (see Chapter 4).

Much of what came to define Green Mountain's unique culture reflected the values, traits, and tough New England work ethic of the people we hired in our formative years. Vermont—a small, mostly rural state with a population of slightly over half a million people in the early 1980s—was an unlikely place to launch a national consumer packaged goods company. But I think that our story and those of friends and neighbors—like ice cream makers Ben Cohen and Jerry Greenfield—show that even from humble roots, with a singular dedication to product, service, people, and a higher purpose, not only can you build category-defining brands, but you can influence the way that others think about business and its opportunity—and obligation—to improve the world.

In 1981, when I founded Green Mountain Coffee Roasters, the world of coffee was new to me—and I set off to learn all that I could about it. But I already knew something about growing a business. In 1971, at the age of 28, I had cofounded a company, Robert Burton Associates, that developed, manufactured, and sold E-Z Wider brand cigarette rolling papers.[13] The name—a pun on the 1969 hippie/biker movie *Easy Rider*—also explained our unique value proposition: papers that were wider than normal papers and easy to roll. The quality of our product, and our creative merchandising and promotions—focused on music and "action sports" events (including race car and hang-gliding sponsorships)—made us a top brand among marijuana smokers. When my partner and I sold the business in 1980, for $6.2 million (equivalent to upward of $22 million in today's market),[14] we had roughly 25 percent of the rolling paper market and were selling over 90 million booklets a year.

As I will detail in Chapter 1, when I first experienced high-quality, fresh-roasted coffee from a local shop in Vermont, I saw a similar opportunity in a new guise—a product so distinctive that it was practically a different beverage from the mass-market coffee I was used to. And like rolling paper, it was a product that satisfied consumers would come back for again and again. I knew that by introducing others to the experience of drinking quality coffee, I would have another hit. (In fact, creating customer experiences with our product eventually became a cornerstone of our marketing.) So with the owners of that little coffee shop, I launched a new business. Eventually, everything I had learned at E-Z Wider—about troubleshooting production lines, optimizing supply chains, and supporting retailers and distribution partners with creative merchandising and promotions—would come to help me at Green Mountain, too. But thanks to the market size for our product—coffee is the second-largest commodity in world—we could have a far broader and more significant impact and opportunity.

A characteristic shared by many founder-entrepreneurs is that we have the kind of mindset that sees opportunities in places that other people overlook. I tried to instill this mindset into the culture of Green Mountain, as well. I encouraged everyone to be alert to opportunities that could help us in a competitive marketplace, which enabled us to identify and develop products that sustained our growth. That's exactly what happened when one of my employees recognized the potential of the single-cup Keurig brewing system and brought it to me. While it flew in the face of conventional industry wisdom at the time, we saw a disruptive opportunity to scale our business. Our company's acquisition of Keurig both disrupted the coffee industry and scaled our profits and impact exponentially (see Chapter 7).

In this book, I will share the business lessons that helped us break out from the specialty coffee pack and achieve stratospheric growth. The story I'll tell is interspersed with lessons in manufacturing inno-vation, multichannel sales, licensing, intellectual property, and M&A strategy. For those in the thriving specialty coffee industry, it's a manual, a secret history. For those outside the industry—the main audience for this book—I believe that Green Mountain's remarkable culture of collaboration, co-creation, personal transformation, and commitment to a greater good provides a model that can be emulated and is more necessary than ever.

Of course, in 30-plus years running a business, there were over-sights and decisions I made that I might have handled differently in retrospect—with more information and insights than I had at the time. I didn't pay enough attention to the culture of our board of direc-tors, especially as the company grew. In retrospect, I see that I could have done more to instill in them a shared sense of our company's mission—of our cultural magic—and encouraged them to participate more fully in our culture of engagement and co-creation, for exam-ple by inviting them to our Appreciative Inquiry summits, where that magic was most on display. I wish I could have shared more such posi-tive experiences with our board.

I also didn't put enough thought into the process of choosing a successor and guiding that person in their new role (see Chapter 8). The challenge of choosing a successor is both common and difficult. In 2022, global CEO turnover reached a five-year high of 11.2 percent, according to the Russell Reynolds Associates Global CEO Turnover Index.[15] And according to McKinsey, more than 90 percent of CEOs say they wish that they had managed their transition differently.[16] The process is even more challenging when someone is taking over from a founder-CEO, who is invested in the company in a different way and tends to manage with a longer view of success in mind. It's important to follow the Better and Better Blueprint not only in the ongoing management of a company, but also when the company is going through vital changes in ownership, leadership, or other major transitions. I found that it was a very different challenge to guide my successor and sustain the company's vision as company chairman rather than CEO, a classic founder's dilemma. In hindsight—after seeing Starbucks hire and fire two CEOs before bringing back Howard Schultz, and former General Electric executive Robert Nardelli radically change (and some would argue, "destroy"[17]) the culture at Home Depot when he succeeded the company's cofounders—I should have seen that choosing a successor to follow through on my vision would be difficult. I wish I had had this book on hand to guide me, and my hope is that it will help others.

It was very challenging to see the company I had grown for three decades change in so many ways, and then, just 2½ years after I left the board, be sold by its new management. But by sharing my reflections on this, I aim to help other founders find ways to ensure that their organization's mission, values, and culture endure beyond them.

My story does not end there. In Chapter 9, I share how what I learned at Green Mountain, and what we all achieved together, continues to reverberate today. Green Mountain's legacy of high-impact work to make the world a better place shows up in the work of numerous former employees and key partners who have become leaders in socially responsible businesses and nonprofit organizations. Through the foundation that I manage with my family, I've worked to bring the transformative engagement that made Green Mountain successful to higher education, helping launch an Appreciative Inquiry business program at Champlain College in Vermont, and supporting the non-profit Let's Grow Kids in advocating for—and getting signed into law—a first-in-the-nation program to make early childcare accessible and affordable for all.

In my life and business, I've come to understand that the more people you can involve in solving a problem, the better the solutions you come up with. And what's more, everyone that you can engage in the process becomes more committed to its success. In writing *Better &Better*, I've turned to many former Green Mountain employees, board members, and other partners to help me recall and reflect on key moments in our company history, to refine the book's vision—and to keep me honest.

In a society that feels increasingly negative, cynical, and divisive, my desire is that this book can shine some hope. Recalling the enthusiasm and happiness of Green Mountain's people working together to build a business and bring positive transformation to all the lives we touched still makes me smile. I will show how we created a genuinely engaged community united by this shared joy in what we were accomplishing together. This is the philosophy and the invitation that I hope business students, entrepreneurs, founders, and organizational leaders will always seek to heed: the possibility that each one of us can always be—and do—better and better.

1

THE NEXT BIG THING

Cultivating an Opportunity Mindset

• •

I f you asked me where I was going in February of 1980, I couldn't have told you exactly. For nearly a decade, I had helped build a lucrative business, Robert Burton Associates, the maker of E-Z Wider rolling papers. From our base in New York City, my cofounder Burton Rubin and I had grown E-Z Wider into one of the most iconic and successful consumer brands to emerge from 1970s counterculture.

I'd met Burt through his wife, Jane Altman, an old family friend. She was the daughter of my father's business partner at Still-Man Manufacturing. He and my father, Paul Stiller, had worked together for 30 years. Our families would have dinner together almost every Sunday. Jane and I had nearly identical childhoods: Our fathers bought the same kinds of cars, the same type of house. And they had kids the same age. Starting the company with Jane's husband felt, in a way, like carrying on a family tradition.

Burt was a trader in specialty metals—along with being a pot enthusiast with dark curly hair and an unmistakable New York accent. Back then, almost everybody rolling a joint took two pieces of rolling paper and glued them together to make a wider paper. We had the idea to create a double-wide paper—and were surprised that no other manufacturer was doing it. Because we focused on providing a quality product, making continuous improvements in manufacturing, and supporting retailers with innovative displays and marketing support, our slow-burning, oversized papers—in their iconic brown-and-white packaging—would come to account for roughly one-quarter of all US cigarette paper sales. We figured out that if we put the individual papers that we sold in one week in a long strip, it would stretch from New York to California and then some. Thinking of that always amazed me, especially when I would fly coast to coast.

The success of E-Z Wider allowed me to enjoy all that Manhattan could offer in the 1970s. My penthouse in an Art Deco building on 22nd Street and Second Avenue boasted glass walls, a wraparound terrace, and a wood-burning fireplace. A couple of prints by Picasso and a few small works by Miró hung on the walls. Before going into the office, I would visit the Midtown Tennis Club, just a few blocks away. On the weekends, I'd take my boat out on the Long Island Sound, or stop by Studio 54, whose co-owner Steve Rubell was a friend of mine from college.

But Burt and I found it more difficult to work together as the years went on and had different visions for the company. I'd tried several times, unsuccessfully, to buy him out, and finally, we'd agreed to put the company up for sale in a private auction. We would sell to the highest bidder and go our separate ways. In reality, though, I was putting together a war chest of a few million dollars—enough, I thought, to make me the winning bidder in the sale. But after several rounds of back-and-forth bidding, an offer from the French cigarette-paper giant Rizla was over what I could afford. It had never occurred to me that I might actually lose the bid.

Now, at the age of 37, I found myself without my company, or a job of any kind. I had just started renovating my Manhattan penthouse—I'd had no plans of leaving the city, after all—and now I needed a place to go as the construction crew moved in. A few years earlier, I'd bought a small condo at Sugarbush Resort, an up-and-coming destination in Warren, Vermont. I took my half of Rizla's check, in the amount of $3.1 million—equivalent to about $10 million today—and hopped on a DC-9 for the 45-minute flight to the nearby Burlington International Airport, where I kept a car for the nearly hourlong drive into the mountains.

I wasn't expecting to find my next business here. I definitely wasn't looking to make a career in coffee. But I knew a great product when I saw one, and when I discovered a tiny café cranking out the best fresh-roasted coffee I'd ever tasted, with people lining up to pay top dollar, it got my attention.

Opportunities come along all the time. You just have to notice them. That's something I learned from my father. I wasn't consciously looking for a new business, but I was always curious and observant, studying new products in the marketplace and new ways that people found for handling everyday problems. My antennae were always up.

Of course, it's not enough to simply notice opportunities. If you want to be successful, you need to move forward on those opportunities, too! Almost by definition, all successful entrepreneurs share what I call an "opportunity mindset," which I define as the ability to perceive and appreciate the positive potential in people, things, and situations, *and* to act purposefully to transform that potential into a positive outcome. They share the determination, and resilience, to make a good idea work.

"Sustain an opportunity mindset" is the first principle in the Better and Better Blueprint, because without this mindset you can never rise above the challenges of starting a business, much less of leading one through years of growth. I remember the advice I got from a lawyer I used to play tennis with in New York. I was thinking about starting E-Z Wider, and I kept going back and forth on the pros and cons, trying to decide if I should pursue it. My lawyer friend asked a clarifying question: What is the worst thing that might happen if I started this business and it didn't work out? I thought about it, and realized, at worst, I would get some really great business experience. But if I didn't go for it, I would always wonder what would have happened. I also remember the advice I got from my dad when I told him about my idea for E-Z Wider. While our company wasn't making anything illegal, I explained, it was associated with marijuana, which was illegal. But he got it. He could see what was happening in the world and saw the opportunity. "Make hay while the sun shines," he said. Most opportunities in business have a "use by" date. Wasting time in endless deliberation is not an option.

When I founded Green Mountain, I had lined up enough funding to get started—though it wouldn't take us as far as I thought. I knew very little, at first, about the coffee business. I didn't have a detailed road map. But I was optimistic and confident I could turn opportunities into outcomes. I was ready to move forward. Embracing the opportunity—and partnering with employees and stakeholders to create a culture of caring and collaboration—I set out on the adventure of a lifetime, meeting people, going places, and changing the way that the world sees business.

STAY OPEN TO OPPORTUNITY

The crisp air and the quiet in Vermont were a big change from New York City. I was an avid skier and passed many days that winter after the sale of E-Z Wider on the slopes—or at a nearby sports center where I'd play tennis or, on occasion, squash or racquetball. I enjoyed the downtime, expecting that I'd head back to New York in a few months, once my apartment was finished.

It's not an exaggeration to say that everything changed one day when I had dinner at the Phoenix Bar & Grill, a restaurant located in a little ski village at the base of the slopes. The Phoenix was co-owned by a former New Yorker named Peter Sussman, and it had excellent food and a big assortment of desserts. Peter was a showman and always did a personal presentation of his desserts, suggesting coffee and after-dinner drink selections to accompany them. I later learned that he focused so much on dessert and coffee not only because they ended the dining experience on an upbeat note, but also because they were the most profitable part of the meal. That night, he sold me on a piece of chocolate-chocolate-chocolate-chip fudge cake—and a life-changing cup of coffee.

At the time, I wasn't much of a coffee drinker. While I enjoyed a morning coffee or espresso or an occasional cup after dinner, I never made it at home. But even so, I could appreciate that the beverage in my mug at the Phoenix was a remarkably different product from the dreck that was being sold in cans at the supermarket. There was a complexity of flavors and smells I'd never noticed before. The Phoenix's menu listed the coffee's source: a local business called Green Mountain Coffee Roasters.

I stopped by the company's store the next day. Green Mountain Coffee Roasters occupied a narrow, rustic building—600 square feet or so—in a strip mall on Route 100 in the town of Waitsfield, Vermont. Upon walking in, you were hit with the smell of just-roasted coffee. A small, noisy roasting machine in the center of the space was cranking out fresh batches of beans. Customers sat around, talking and sipping just-brewed coffee, atop big burlap sacks of raw beans piled up against the walls. Along with a standard BUNN pour-over brewer, the store had a beautiful copper La Pavoni machine from Italy, which it used for pulling espressos and foaming milk for the store's decadent hot chocolate.

On counters made of wide barnboard, glass apothecary jars show-cased two to three dozen types of fresh-roasted beans. A chalkboard listed the coffees' exotic origins—Cameroon, Uganda, New Guinea—and their prices, which made an even bigger impression. I was amazed to watch people shop at the little supermarket across the way—where they could buy Maxwell House or Folgers for about $3 a pound—put their groceries in their car, and then make a special trip to buy coffee at Green Mountain for about $7 a pound. No one batted an eye. I bought a pound to bring home. Carrying the paper bag, warm in my hands from the just-roasted beans inside, was like bringing home fresh bread from the bakery. More than just the intoxicating aroma of fresh-roasted coffee, I smelled opportunity.

Green Mountain, I found out, had been started in 1979 by Doug and Jamie Balne, a well-liked couple in their late twenties who'd moved to the area from Connecticut so they could ski more. Doug—who sported longish brown hair, a permanent tan, and a smile that earned him the nickname "Rainbow Dougy"—had been a Minor League Baseball pitcher until his career was cut short by injury. I recognized him from the racquetball court. His wife, Jamie—athletic, with dark brown hair and a big smile—was equally magnetic.

Before starting the business, Doug had worked as a Realtor, and Jamie was a schoolteacher. Back in Connecticut, Doug had also been helping his brother roast coffee and sell it to business customers—the industry term for this is "office coffee service." When the Balnes moved to Vermont, they continued to get personal shipments of fresh-roasted coffee from Doug's brother; and when they served it to dinner guests, the response was something like mine at the Phoenix. They went crazy for it, and Doug kept bumping up the size of the order from his brother to meet all his requests from locals.

Sugarbush was gaining a reputation as a destination for second-home owners from New York and Boston, and it boasted a handful of upscale restaurants. But the Balnes had identified something that was missing: great coffee. So with coaching from Doug's brother, they found themselves starting a little roasting company of their own, building their operation around a new kind of coffee roaster made by Sivetz.

The Sivetz fluid-bed roaster could prepare about 30 pounds of coffee beans at a time, roasting them at temperatures ranging from 400 to 500 degrees (Fahrenheit). Using a gas heater and a fan, it roasted the beans on a bed of air, rather than turning them on a circular tray beneath a heat source, as other small-batch roasting machines did. It allowed for more fine tuning during the roasting process. Making each batch of coffee took about 20 minutes, with a fine misting of water at the end of the cycle to cool the beans down. Loud and constantly requiring maintenance, the Sivetz nonetheless made great coffee when everything was working. And most important, because it was small enough to have right inside the store, it allowed the Balnes to sell roasted beans at their peak of freshness, before they started losing their distinctive flavor elements. That, to me, was the real innovation in the Balnes' business model. Freshness.

I became a Green Mountain regular, replenishing my stash of fresh-roasted beans and getting to know the Balnes and their business. We take it for granted today, but in the early 1980s, good coffee wasn't something that most people had been exposed to yet. Companies including Peet's Coffee were fresh-roasting high-quality "second-wave" coffee on the West Coast, with a dark roast profile, but they were still relatively small and regional. On the East Coast, George Howell at the Coffee Connection in Boston and Donald Schoenholt at Gillies in New York City were selling high-quality fresh-roasted coffee locally by the late 1970s. But for the average coffee drinker everyplace else, the biggest choice they had to make was picking the red can (Folgers) or the blue can (Maxwell House).

The coffee I had discovered in Vermont was an objectively better product. It was made from carefully roasted arabica beans, not the indifferently treated, cheaper robusta beans that big commercial brands used. It occurred to me that if other people like me—casual morning-coffee drinkers—could just get a taste of the good stuff, they'd be converted, too. And even more important, I realized that regular coffee drinkers would upgrade to a better-tasting product if given the opportunity. American coffee drinking habits had been stagnant a long time.

I was looking for a new business, and I could see that what the Balnes were doing at a small scale in their little roaster could be a model for something bigger. In addition to the retail business, they'd also started selling wholesale, to restaurant accounts like the Phoenix, and had brought in Dan Cox—one of my pickup racquetball partners—to help grow that side of things. I saw opportunities not only to increase sales through these existing channels, but to expand beyond them, too.

I had an intuition that here was an opportunity that could be even bigger than E-Z Wider rolling papers. But I didn't just trust my intuition—I did a lot of research, too. When I take an interest in something, I tend to study it obsessively. I have always been a voracious reader, and over the next several months, as I considered my next moves, I read everything I could on coffee and the coffee industry and looked for data to support my vision.

When making a decision like this, you also need to seek out others' opinions. That doesn't mean you have to act on all the advice you get! Not everyone can see the vision. For example, when I solicited the opinion of a friend—a sought-after marketing consultant who had run Maxwell House for a couple of years—he didn't think I would be able to convert enough coffee drinkers to a more upscale product and compete in a crowded market. He encouraged me to save my money by skipping the investment. His pessimism didn't change my mind, though. Dave hadn't experienced the coffee firsthand, after all.

When I looked at Green Mountain, I was intrigued and excited by the similarities between roasting coffee and my previous business, making rolling papers. With E-Z Wider, Burt and I had recognized a sizable market—a burgeoning subculture of marijuana smokers in the 1970s—that was underserved by traditional consumer packaged goods brands. We knew this from observing that a lot of pot smokers were crafting solutions themselves—gluing two small cigarette papers together to create a wider one that was easier for rolling marijuana. Being present to what was going on, figuring out what customers needed, and giving it to them seemed like common sense. My cofounder and I couldn't believe that no one else had thought of the same thing. Maybe they did. But we made it happen!

Like rolling papers, coffee was a consumable product, something that people need to keep buying again and again. Compared with a durable-products business, consumables companies see steadier revenue streams and repeat customers. If you can really develop a better product, you get a customer who keeps coming back. At the Balnes' store, I'd seen that when people were offered a better alternative—even a considerably more expensive one—they lined up for it.

In early 1981, I started to have serious talks with the Balnes about expanding their coffee concept. If I could buy their business, I knew I could take Green Mountain Coffee Roasters to the next level. I was probably feeling a bit flush, thanks to the E-Z Wider sale. But I'd done my research, too. And I understood the risks.

Historical data from the US Bureau of Labor Statistics shows that about half of all new businesses fail within five years; only about 25 percent make it to 15 years or more.[1] Other research shows that just 1 of every 12 companies move from being an average performer to a top-quintile performer over a 10-year period.[2] At the time, I wasn't aware of these bad odds. But even if I had been, like many entrepreneurs, I was self-confident and optimistic and was willing to take the risk.

In the spring, the Balnes and I agreed on a purchase price, and for about $100,000—roughly equivalent to their total sales in the previous year—I acquired the business outright. In April 1981, I re-incorporated it as Green Mountain Coffee Roasters Inc. and distributed shares in the company three ways, among myself, Doug Balne, and Morris Webster, my former CFO from E-Z Wider, whom I'd asked to come and head operations, as I was expecting to be more of a silent partner. A little more than a year after getting out of E-Z Wider, I was in business again.

SHARE A POSITIVE GUIDING VISION

You'll never be successful in business if you can't really *see* yourself being successful in business. I always had the vision that we would be successful. To help me realize that vision, as I took over at Green Mountain, I leaned on a formula of sorts that I'd learned from my father, who had been a successful manufacturer of tubular heating elements: Make the best-quality product, provide the best service, and take care of your employees. Like many simple rules, these are harder to follow than they sound. But as I started to reckon with what it really meant to scale up a specialty coffee roaster, I let them guide me. And over time, I built on them, finding a formula of my own, rooted in my father's wisdom.

Being "forward-looking" is consistently ranked one of the most important characteristics in a leader—in a large-scale survey of working people around the world published by professors from the Santa Clara Leavey School of Business, 72 percent listed "being forward-looking" as a trait they wanted in a leader.[3] (The only trait they rated more important was "honesty.") Being forward-looking is essential to maintaining an opportunity mindset—you really need to believe in a successful future state to make the kinds of investments and sacrifices that are necessary in the startup phase of just about any organization.

The kind of vision that it takes to launch new products and services in untested markets can make successful entrepreneurs seem delusional when they're starting out. Think of Steve Jobs talking about the massive potential in "personal" computers in the late 1970s. Or Nike cofounder Phil Knight's belief that the future of athletic footwear lay in obscure Japanese track shoes. Or the cofounders of the beverage company Guayakí, known for its yerba mate. It took 13 years for the company to reach $10 million in annual sales, but on the *How I Built This* podcast, cofounder David Karr says, "It was always a really big vision . . . we were going to be a billion-dollar business. There was never a long-term concern; it was just how we get through this next valley."[4] Today, Guayakí has sales of more than $200 million a year, making it a big player in the booming alternative-beverage market. Yerba mate spoke to Karr the way that small-batch, freshly roasted arabica coffee spoke to me. In both cases, it took the rest of the world a little while to "get it."

The kind of vision I'm talking about is, essentially, the ability to create a strong mental image of what you want to attain and how you are going to attain it. It just makes sense that when it comes to *any-thing* you want in life, it really helps if you can envision it this way. Complementing that internal mental image with external physical imagery—such as a photo relevant to what you're contemplating—can be immensely helpful. Over the years, I have come to understand more and more just how effective visualization and affirmation are in realizing goals and effecting change.

At some point while running E-Z Wider, I had read about people cutting up pictures and putting them in a file or pinning them up on the wall as a way of manifesting them. It didn't make sense to me at the time, but I figured "Why not?" and gave it a try. As I learned more, studying among other techniques the Silva Method of meditation and visualization, and productivity guru David Allen's use of multisensory imagery to realize goals, I came to rely more and more on visualization as a sort of secret power. Like effective advertising, visualizations and positive affirmations can influence your thinking, and ultimately your actions. With a clear picture of what you want, you start to bring in other elements, consciously and unconsciously, that help to manifest it. In fact, research has shown that people who just write down their goals are up to 40 percent more likely to achieve them than those who don't.[5]

My pictures on the wall in the early 1980s included a North American Sabreliner business jet. As years went by, I added a house on the Intracoastal Waterway in Florida, a large yacht, and other things. It also included—as sort of a lark at the time—the cover of a *Forbes* magazine "Billionaires" issue. As Green Mountain experienced a string of money-losing years after I took over, my confidence took some hits. Far from becoming billionaires, we were barely keeping our shirts. But by the mid-1990s, Green Mountain was doing well enough that I was actually able to purchase a plane—a twin-engine Beechcraft Baron. Soon after, I was even approached by someone interested in selling a half interest in a plane that she owned: a Sabreliner! Was that just a coincidence? About 20 years later, I purchased a house on the Intracoastal Waterway, which looked a lot like the one in the picture I'd pinned to my wall. What's more, the Realtor who sold us the house was the same one in the picture I'd hung up—something I only realized months later when clearing out old files. Finally, in 2011, some 15 years after I stuck the magazine cover to my wall, I also made the *Forbes* billionaires list.

I encouraged people I worked with to use visualization, too. I remember a woman who worked in Green Mountain customer service early on. She was overseeing a department of about eight people when she put up an inspiring picture above her desk—of a huge call center with 150 customer reps on the phone. Ultimately, her department would get even bigger than that!

Along with visualization, positive self-talk is another way to bolster your chances of success. (I talk more about these techniques in Chapter 5.) In the 1970s, while studying the Silva Method, I learned about Émile Coué, a French psychologist and pharmacist who helped develop the practice of positive psychology in the early 1900s. Coué taught that what you believe, you can make real—and that if you said something enough times, you would end up believing it. A good example of this is Coué's personal affirmation: "Every day in every way, life is getting better and better." I abbreviated that and adopted it as a sort of mantra in my early years running Green Mountain. If someone asked how I was doing, I'd respond, "Better and better!" And I believed it.

My wife, Christine, still remembers how, in the early years at Green Mountain, I would often lie awake at night repeating the specific revenue and profit numbers I wanted the company to hit six months out, a year out, and even further in the future: "In three years, we'll do this much product, and it will cost this much . . ." In saying it aloud, I was, in an important sense, committing myself to making it real.

Bringing a positive mindset to any business pursuit is critical. In Shawn Achor's inspiring book *Before Happiness*, he explains that people tend to see the world in ways that confirm their fundamental beliefs about it. "That reality is the key to everything," he writes. "It is what lets you see opportunities instead of obstacles, new roads instead of dead ends, paths to success instead of failure." Achor shows how you can develop a mindset, and a set of skills, that he calls "positive genius."[6] When you cultivate this can-do outlook, you'll see and be empowered by incredible new opportunities.

Research supports the idea that confident, optimistic founders and CEOs create more value—and better, happier workplaces, too. A 2007 study in *International Coaching Psychology Review* by Dana Arakawa and Margaret Greenberg found that optimism in business leaders (measured by an assessment called the Life Orientation Test Revised) correlates significantly with employee optimism and project performance.[7] A 2021 study by researchers from DePaul University and Stevens Institute of Technology examined CEO option-exercise behavior—whether they took advantage of opportunities to purchase stock at a discount or not—as an indicator of optimism; it found that CEO optimism results in an additional value of roughly 17 to 23 percent.[8] The "optimism premium," they write, is greater in firms that are in more competitive industries, have higher cash flow volatility, and have higher R&D expenditures. Yet as I write, CEO pessimism is the norm. In PwC's Annual Global CEO Survey for 2023, only 42 percent are "very confident" or "extremely confident" in their own company's prospects for the next year—and 40 percent don't think their companies will be economically viable in a decade if they continue on their current path.[9]

As the founder of an organization, it's not enough just to have a positive, clear vision and an optimistic outlook. You also need to share it with others—customers, investors, shareholders, and especially employees. As I aimed to transform the coffee roaster I'd just bought from a $100,000-per-year business into a multimillion-dollar business, I was committed to finding and working with like-minded people and, with them, creating a shared vision for the future. But first, I needed to get them in the door.

As I interviewed early employees and told them what I wanted to achieve—building a Fortune 500 company from the ground up, right here in Vermont, by roasting coffee—I'm confident that more than a few people walked out of my cluttered office thinking, "That guy's crazy." However, most of them ended up coming to work with me. I wasn't thinking small—and if I could actually do what I said, who wouldn't want to get in on the ground floor of something that big? But you have to put the vision out there.

I never wanted the vision of our company to be mine alone. Rather, I believed it was something to be developed collectively with employees. Even the very best ideas I've come up with on my own get better when I've shared them with others and incorporated their feedback.

From early on at Green Mountain, we'd bring people together for group exercises focused on imagining the future together. A prompt might be something like: *Imagine that we have made the cover of* Fortune. *What does the accompanying article say about how we became so successful?* That and similar exercises helped us to identify high points we could aim for in the future, informing the collective vision and engaging people in making it a reality. Throughout the following chapters, I'll describe many more ways that we invited employees to co-create Green Mountain's vision, deciding where we were going and how we would get there, together.

HARNESS THE POWER OF INTENTION

Although both creating a vision of what you want to achieve and sharing and growing the vision with others' help are necessary first steps in launching any enterprise, what brings ultimate success is your day-to-day work. When you focus on the present moment and getting things done the best you can, the future takes care of itself. You discover the "how" along the way. Getting too fixated on the specific way you get from here to there only limits your possibilities. If something is not working well, you simply need to try something else. Reality is too unpredictable to predetermine exactly how you'll pull off any given task or initiative. There was so much that I couldn't foresee in the first couple of years of our business.

I didn't foresee, for example, that in the first few years of the company's existence, I would lose both of my initial partners. Or that on a trip to New York, I'd go on a date with my ex-girlfriend Connie's best friend, Christine—and end up marrying her about six months later. Or that we would have wonderful children together in the next several years. Or that I'd be working days and nights in a ramshackle office above a restaurant in a Vermont strip mall, with Christine doing manual spreadsheets using a calculator in the tiny conference room. Or that instead of being a silent partner as I'd planned, I'd be the very active CEO of a money-losing coffee roaster.

I think this is where the power of intention comes in. Deepak Chopra talks about the difference between desire and intention in his book *The Seven Spiritual Laws of Success*, which I read almost daily in the 1990s. I would refer readers to that book for a fuller explanation, but one point struck me in particular: that so many people desire something in life, but it eludes them. People who have an intention to realize something are more likely to be successful—either consciously or subconsciously they develop an inner confidence, "knowing" that their goal will be achieved. Think of *The Little Engine That Could*—intention is the difference between "I think I can" and "I know I can."

Having a strong intention helps you to achieve and maintain a state of flow more often, allowing you to figure things out dynamically, reacting to events without letting them knock you off course. It supports your ability to transform possibilities into positive outcomes, part of sustaining an opportunity mindset.

Starting a business is not unlike flying. I got my pilot's license while I was at Syracuse University, and joined the flying club at my next school, Parsons College in Iowa. I remember once taking off in a torrential downpour in a plane I was piloting. I really couldn't see anything. This is unnerving for a passenger, but it's minor for a pilot. You line up the plane on the runway, set your gyrocompass to the right heading, and just follow that setting as you take off, flying blindly into the rain. You can fly from one place to the next without seeing anything. You just have to believe the instruments and trust the data you're receiving along the way.

In business, you're often flying blind, but if you know where you're going and your intention is set, you get there. Vision and intention, together, are what help leaders to sustain a long-term effort. And a group intention, which comes out of creating goals together, is much stronger than the intention of one individual alone. By cocreating strategies and setting goals with employees, you start out with an agreement, not instructions handed down from a leader. The collective intention that resulted when we engaged everyone at Green Mountain was key to the success we ultimately achieved.

When I bought the Balnes' business and incorporated Green Mountain Coffee Roasters in April 1981, I hadn't worked out all the details of becoming a specialty coffee powerhouse, a pioneer in corporate social responsibility, or an award-winning workplace. I was simply focused on the considerable work in front of us: producing high-quality coffee as efficiently as possible, understanding and enhancing the consumer's experience and appreciation of our product, supporting partners in wholesale, and creating a workplace that took care of our employees. First, though, I had to put out some fires.

LESSONS TO GO

Trust your experience. It was a compelling personal experience—backed up by formal and informal market research—that convinced me of the big opportunity in rolling papers and again in specialty coffee.

Look for what's missing. The discovery of an existing workaround—for instance, pot smokers gluing together several rolling papers for a joint—can point to hidden market opportunities.

Advertise to yourself. Use vision boards and multisensory cues for inspiration. In the best of all possible worlds, what will things look like, and what will you accomplish?

Imagine you've already been successful. How did you do it? What were some of the most important first steps you took? Be as specific as possible.

Stay positive. Numerous studies show that more optimistic CEOs run happier, more profitable organizations.

Check the compass. Business plans and strategies need to adapt and evolve—surprises and detours are inevitable. But successful leaders navigate through these changes with a steady internal compass and a clear destination in mind.

2

BETTER AND BETTER

Inspiring the Co-creation of Excellence

• •

As an entrepreneur, it was essential to commit fully to the venture I was launching. Being a passive observer is not an option when it comes to building a successful business. To engage all your employees and stakeholders in the pursuit of excellence, you need to be all in, not sitting on the sidelines. This lesson became painfully clear to me soon after I'd acquired Green Mountain from the Balnes.

As I began pursuing a strategy to grow the Green Mountain Coffee Roasters brand in both retail and wholesale channels, we hit obstacle after obstacle, any of which might have stopped us in our tracks. But our shared commitment to the quality of our product, and to caring for one another, sustained us and laid the foundation for the transformative workplace culture and wildly successful business we would become. This chapter illustrates how the co-creation of excellence became a pillar of our business, and a second key element in the Better and Better Blueprint.

BE ALL IN, OR GET OUT

In the first year or so after buying Green Mountain, I was content to work in the background, studying the coffee industry and developing and directing strategy. I left others to figure out most of the details of making it all work.

Doug and Jamie Balne, who'd started the coffee business in 1979, would continue to oversee everything having to with roasting. Dan Cox—the outgoing former college counselor and formidable racquetball player whom the Balnes had recently hired—would lead our sales efforts and become the face of the business, a relief to me, since I was not that comfortable being the center of attention nor doing public speaking. To oversee day-to-day company operations, I brought in a former colleague from E-Z Wider. I hoped to create another successful company that would sustain my lifestyle and, one day, allow me to provide for a family. But as my new business started going off the rails, I realized that it was naïve to think I could do this from a distance.

When I purchased the business from the Balnes, it had annual revenues of about $120,000, including retail sales and restaurant accounts. Now, as we invested to grow the business, we were burning through money. In the first few years, I estimate we lost somewhere around $1.5 million.

As I dug into our operations at Green Mountain, trying to figure out where our losses were coming from, I discovered that my other partner, whom I'd brought from E-Z Wider, had been helping himself to the company's money. Rather than taking him to court, I bought out his share of the business and he left town. I'd put a lot of trust in him and considered him a friend. So this betrayal stung.

My life was changing, too. In 1983, I married Christine, a flight attendant based in New York. We'd known each other for years and only started dating after I'd bought Green Mountain. Christine started to make the commute to Vermont with me every couple of weeks, and ended up pitching in at our office above the Fiddler's on the Green restaurant. After our daughter, Jules, was born later that year, we started to make the drive at night, so that Jules could sleep in her car seat most of the way. But by the time Jules was five or six months old, my penthouse was starting to feel crowded, and the six-hour commute between the city and the mountains of Vermont was getting old.

In early 1983, the Balnes decided to get out of the partnership. I bought their shares in the company, and they moved to Florida. Two years after starting a company where I had two partners, I was now the only one left to make my dream of launching a successful national coffee brand a reality. At this point, I couldn't afford to hire someone else to run the company, and I questioned whether that would work, anyway. When you own a business, you bring a much higher level of motivation and creativity to figuring out a path to success. To protect my investment, I had to go from president of the company in name only, to "president in action."

Looking back, it was probably the best thing that could have happened. It forced me to dig into parts of the business I might never have really understood otherwise, to appreciate all that went into our operations and where we could improve. Being on the front line—making things happen rather than simply making investments—brought me a sense of excitement and fulfillment that was different, too.

When you're the leader of a company in startup mode—asking your employees to go above and beyond all the time—people want to know that you're working as hard as they are. That can lead to high levels of stress and anxiety in business founders, and can sometimes lead to an unfortunate glorification of working long hours for its own sake. For several years in the 1980s, I did work a lot of 12-to-14-hour days. I wasn't trying to set an example for anyone. I was energized, and I worked long hours to get things done and figure out what worked best. But I wouldn't suggest that working so hard is the most effective way to do things; it is clearly not. Research shows that working more than 40 hours a week can lead to decreased productivity—as well as medical and psychological problems and injuries.[1]

To be sure, balancing a startup and a young family was a serious challenge. It's one that many founders will be familiar with. One of the leading causes of divorce is financial stress—something entrepreneurs understand all too well. Even as I poured my money from the sale of E-Z Wider—as well as funds from the sale of my Manhattan penthouse and artworks I had invested in—into Green Mountain, the company continued to lose money. I began to worry about our finances, as I was now supporting not only myself, but my wife and daughter. But Christine was very supportive and helpful. She understood my vision for the business and—after the many nights we were kept awake by my projections of future revenues—my intention to succeed.

CREATE AN EXPERIENCE, NOT JUST A PRODUCT

As I plotted a strategy for Green Mountain, I wanted to reinvent how Americans drink and enjoy their coffee—and I wanted to make us a major national brand. To achieve these ambitious goals, Green Mountain Coffee would need to be everywhere, available both at retail stores and through a thriving wholesale business. While building our own chain of cafés to introduce consumers to our brand, we would need to court new wholesale customers among restaurants, hotels, bed and breakfasts, gas stations, and—most important—supermarkets, where the majority of coffee for home consumption was sold.

I knew we had an objectively better product than what most people were drinking. But the only way for consumers to know that was to get them to experience it—in as many ways as possible. My belief in the incomparable power of sharing positive experiences as a means of creating understanding and transforming mindsets became a foundational principle of Green Mountain's business, guiding our retail and wholesale businesses, as well as our internal employee development programs.

To help consumers taste high-quality, freshly roasted coffee, though, we had to create a firsthand in-store experience that would be wholly new—at least in the United States in the early 1980s. When I bought Green Mountain in 1981, there was no template for a retail coffee experience. Americans didn't spend time in European-style cafés—this was still a few years before Starbucks started its nationwide expansion outside Seattle—and that was never our model. To get people to appreciate our coffee, I felt they needed to have an experience like the one customers had coming into the roaster in Waterbury, Vermont, sitting on stools or on a burlap sack amid the aromatic notes of roasting beans and a great selection of roasted coffees. I wanted consumers to see us as coffee experts who could help them have the ultimate coffee experience. If we could reproduce that experience regionally and then maybe nationally, I believed we could build a huge market for our coffee. What I didn't see was how difficult it would be to maintain this operationally challenging (and often expensive) part of the business.

Soon after I bought Green Mountain, we—the leadership group of Doug, Morris, Dan Cox, and I—decided to open a new store in Winooski, a suburb of Burlington just over the hill from the University of Vermont. It was in a historic mill building on the Winooski River, and I wanted it to be a showcase for the brand that would offer a coffee experience that hit all the senses.

The store would have roasters that cranked out fresh beans all day long—just like the original shop in Waitsfield. But I was convinced that we needed to have good food, too. I didn't think that coffee, on its own, was enough of a draw. Sure, we'd had some home-baked brownies and such at the original shop, but for the new Winooski café/restaurant, I wanted more. At a fancy food show, Doug and I discovered a franchise called Vie de France, which supplied us with incredible frozen croissants, and we baked our own sour cream coffee cake and chocolate-chunk cookies from scratch. From the time the shop opened in September 1981, people from the Burlington community embraced it. It was always one of our best-performing locations, and it became a second home for my kids.

In 1984, we opened another, even bigger store in Portland, Maine. Setting up in another market so far from our home base was a big challenge. And it was not what we originally intended. We'd had a connection with a local person in the wholesale coffee business who wanted to partner with us and run a store there. After we'd scouted retail locations and developed plans, when it came time to sign the lease and put down the funds, the person backed out. But having done all this research and feeling ready to go, we decided to give it a whirl. The opportunity mindset kicked in, and I saw we could transform this apparent problem into an opportunity—even if the store presented more of a learning opportunity than an immediate financial success. As far as we knew, there wasn't yet a significant specialty coffee roaster in Maine, and if we could replicate what we'd done in Vermont, it would give us a foothold in another part of New England.

This was, architecturally, one of the coolest-looking coffee stores in the country at the time. It was huge—about 4,000 square feet. It had a scratch kitchen, and friends with a bagel business in Vermont helped us set up our own bagel bakery. It ran about 20 hours a day, with the bagel bakers coming in to start their shift at two or three in the morning. The bakers, we discovered, were their own subspecies, waking up in the middle of the night and leaving at noon, yelling and screaming as they worked in their steam-room surroundings. No one had any clue what "cost control" meant. And the economics of the bagel business, we discovered, were challenging. At some point, we did the math and realized we would need to sell some 66 dozen bagels a day to break even. Even on our best days, we weren't doing those kinds of numbers. So we started wholesaling bagels—a long story in its own right. And a distraction from our main business, which was supposed to be selling coffee.

The Portland store—like nearly all the stores we'd eventually open—roasted its coffee on site. For most people, the multisensory experience of seeing, hearing, and smelling coffee beans being roasted, ground, and brewed, of walking out holding a warm, fresh bag, was entirely new. Until then, there had been a disconnect between the coffee in your cup and where it came from. A lot of people didn't even know what roasting coffee smelled like. Our stores also stocked every brewing machine, coffee pot, and container known to man: Turkish coffee pots, Neapolitan flip coffee pots, stainless steel coffee flasks. These weren't real moneymakers, but they added to the total experience. They made people excited about the whole world of coffee, and they gave us added credibility as the coffee experts.

While our stores succeeded in exposing customers to our brand and in starting to build a community around coffee, they were difficult to operate. There was high turnover and lots of waste, and you could never keep things clean enough. The glass jars that we used for storing fresh-roasted beans needed to be washed out constantly. They would often break, and we'd have to throw out all the coffee inside. And cooking from scratch was expensive and labor-intensive. Our Portland café had a half dozen or so pastry chefs, which would have been a lot for a bakery but for an independent coffee joint was ridiculous. We were learning hard but valuable lessons about the difficulties involved in launching retail—and wholesale—operations so far from our home base.

Thankfully, our wholesale business was taking off as we gained restaurant, hospitality, and business accounts all around Vermont and beyond. In 1986, we acquired our first major supermarket customer, Kings Food Markets, a high-end grocer with about 20 stores then in New Jersey. This would be our first million-dollar account, and we got it because an executive from Kings came into our Portland store while vacationing in Maine. That deal alone practically justified the hassles of running that store.

In my effort to maximize channels for experiencing Green Mountain Coffee, in 1987, we hired Rick Peyser, a compact and energetic marathon runner who came from a direct mail and retail business called Garden Way, to expand our mail-order business. The Waitsfield community had a lot of second-home owners from New York and Boston, and the idea was that they'd come to Vermont for skiing, take our coffee home, and get on our mailing list for home delivery. Rick used to put out a call when he had a big mailing to get out, recruiting people from across our company to help lick stamps. That's how high tech we were then!

Dan Cox, head of sales, knew that as a young business, building a reputation with key influencers would be crucial for our company. We didn't have the advertising budget of Maxwell House or Folgers. But we had a VIP list of people that we'd send free coffee to—a pound a month, no strings attached. Our hope was that they'd enjoy the coffee at home and talk it up in their circles. The free-coffee list included Ben Cohen and Jerry Greenfield, our Vermont congressional delegation, the authors Stephen King and John Irving, Supreme Court Justice Sandra Day O'Connor, and many local teachers, police, and firefighters. The *New Yorker* magazine cartoonist and Vermonter Ed Koren was another Green Mountain VIP. He showed his appreciation by sending Christmas cards and occasional signed drawings, which he allowed us to make into small cards that we used for thank you notes. That was quite a coup for a tiny company with no marketing budget.

By cultivating a base of customers who loved and believed in us, we were soon able to establish ourselves as a leading brand in the industry. Investing thoughtfully in relationships with potential influencers doesn't have to cost much, and you never know what it might lead to. In this case, we got to share the fun and unexpected experience of receiving a gift from an award-winning cartoonist with our partners and customers.

HIRE FOR MINDSET AND LET PEOPLE GROW

Starting a company in Vermont, I benefited from tapping into a remarkable pool of local talent and a community whose values would help define our workplace culture. We weren't big enough, nor did I have enough money, to lure a lot of specialized talent from Boston or New York. So almost everyone we hired in the first few years came from the area around Waterbury, near two local ski areas, Sugarbush and Stowe. But Waterbury was soon to be home to two of Vermont's fastest-growing companies: Green Mountain Coffee Roasters and Ben & Jerry's, which opened its first factory there in 1985.

Central Vermont is rural Vermont. There was a particular mindset. People had a solid work ethic, but local traditions also had to be respected. The time leading up to Christmas was always busy for us. It was also deer season, which was a religion in the area. We adjusted schedules to make sure that the work got done, and so that people could also get out to deer camp. We didn't really have a choice!

"The Vermont way" also meant doing right by your neighbors and lending a hand when needed. As a leader, I was able to nurture that spirit—supporting one another was an understood Green Mountain value from the outset. When someone at the company had a house that was burned in a fire in the late 1980s, 20 or 30 employees went out there to help the person clean up. Mike Pelchar remembers calling in for the day off on his third day of work, in 1987. His young child had been running a fever for a few days, and it was his turn to stay home while his wife went to her job. Mike was a conscientious guy, and since he'd barely started working for us, he was worried about missing a day. He was pretty surprised when, later in the morning, his manager, Dan Cox, showed up at his house with a few boxes of tissues and some cold medicine.

"I never forgot that act of kindness," Mike later told me. "That was my introduction to Green Mountain." Sharing and celebrating these kinds of stories helped establish Green Mountain's early culture. By "modeling" caring actions, we reinforced the idea that, in a real sense, we were an extended family as much as a company. In these early days of the business, I could already see how seeking high points, which would become one of my Better and Better Blueprint principles, was so important to building and sustaining a winning company culture.

The key people who ran the company with me through our first decade were all, like me, coffee industry neophytes who had to learn on the job. Most had never even had the type of role that I hired them for. Our plant manager, Curtis Hooper, had never run a production facility before. Dan Cox—who, as I've already mentioned, was the face of the business in our formative years and an early vice president of the company—had been a college counselor before going into sales with us. Steve Sabol, an introverted intellectual with an industrial arts degree and some experience in property management, became an unlikely sales star, in addition to playing an instrumental role in our acquisition of Keurig. Patty Vincent, one of our first employees, had been a server at the Common Man restaurant in Warren, Vermont. She first came to work at our original retail store in Waitsfield, and later she headed up key organic coffee initiatives at the company.

Part of sustaining an opportunity mindset is recognizing the potential in people. What they may have lacked in formal coffee industry experience, Green Mountain's early employees made up for in their commitment to continuous improvement; they were always learning and looking for ways to further their abilities and help the performance of the organization.

Allowing people to find the best way forward by themselves not only helped them to develop skills and confidence; it made us a stronger, more resilient company. Nobody knew how we were going to accomplish what we wanted to do. But at the same time, we had no self-imposed limitations. Building a national brand is a lofty goal, and there is not one particular way to do it. We were never burdened by people saying, "This is the way we've always done it."

For the first few years, I was part of the interview process for many candidates. For new businesses, which typically can't compete on things like compensation and benefits with established companies, a personal pitch from the founder can be the most effective way to sway a job candidate. Who better to paint the picture of your organization's vision and to bring new hires into company communication channels? For that reason, I think every founder should consider interviewing as one of their essential tasks. Like most other decisions affecting the company, though, I wanted hiring to be a group process. Having multiple people interview job candidates demonstrated to candidates the way that we worked together as a team, and it showed our employees that their involvement mattered. If employees were involved in hiring someone, I felt they would also be more invested in seeing that person develop within the company. They wanted "their" people to be successful, even if the final hiring decision was always up to the new employee's direct manager.

In hiring, I tended to put more faith in the quality of a person than on expertise, making decisions based on attitude and personality. Of course, when I needed particular skills, I wouldn't hire someone who didn't have them. But for many jobs in the organization—and I'm sure at many other companies, especially in the startup stage—specific skills are less important than commitment and engagement with the company's vision and values. Over time, we would get more sophisticated with our hiring process as well as our training programs, and I personally attended numerous conferences and workshops to stay current on the best practices in human resources.

Not everyone found the exact right job in the company right away. If things did not work out, but the person was a good employee, we'd look for a better fit. As preemployment job simulations have shown, you learn far more from watching someone handle a job than you ever could in an interview. I encouraged people to "own" their job areas, and I gave employees in training lots of leeway to solve problems themselves. The people who stayed with the company were those who appreciated the autonomy, who thrived on the responsibility, and who were always ready to try something new. We see this in other successful startups that have experienced exponential growth, including Netflix, where cofounder and former CEO Reed Hastings promoted a "No Rules" policy that aims to remove controls and allow high performers to be innovative.[2]

When you hire folks for a can-do attitude, don't be surprised when they get things done. A great example is Mike Bickford, "Bick," who was in his mid-twenties when he joined us to drive a delivery route that covered important new accounts with wholesale customers in Boston and New York. Bick was an old-school ski bum, fair-skinned with dark hair and a deep, booming voice, who lived in the Mad River Valley and happened to have the two main qualifications we needed: a driver's license and lots of experience in winter driving conditions. More important, he was friendly, outgoing, and helpful.

Bick and his big blue van loaded with coffee would leave Waterbury on a Tuesday and come back on a Thursday night, hitting 20 or more customers, including restaurants, specialty stores, and groceries on a route that covered over 700 miles. The job was a lot more complicated than just dumping off coffee at the stores. They all needed specific delivery times, and you'd have to account for traffic, weather, and other variables. Bick figured out all the logistics on his own way before GPS and Google Maps. He loaded the truck on Tuesday evenings, left Vermont around 4 a.m., and drove to New Jersey, delivering to 15 or so Kings grocery accounts, and then he stopped for the night. The next day, he went into Manhattan, delivered to the Harvard Club and other key accounts, and got back home late Thursday or early Friday. In addition to assisting customers as they inspected his shipments upon delivery, Bick had to stock the coffee, rotating out any old inventory. The relationships he built really helped us retain accounts, and he was one of the most passionate guys we hired, staying with the company for 16 years.

Paul Comey—a local expert on woodstoves whom I brought in as a consultant to help with air pollution at our facility in the early 1980s—had what amounted to the longest on-the-job interview in Green Mountain history. A jack-of-all-trades with dark hair thinning on top, Paul was a born problem solver who became a fixture around Green Mountain, helping us deal with one equipment emergency after another. He liked working as his own contractor, but by 1993—the year Green Mountain went public—we needed him full time, and I hired him as our executive director of facilities and process engineering. By then, I knew what we were getting. And he knew exactly what he was in for!

Trying out a variety of different jobs was something that happened organically at Green Mountain, especially during our first decade of business; and there were many people who would take any job just to get in the door, because they knew our reputation in the community. But other companies have formalized the practice of trying out jobs. Dutch brewer Heineken, for example, has a job rotation program that lets college graduates rotate through departments, including packaging, product development, brewing, and quality assurance, to get a feeling for the work.[3] After completing the program, they can join the department that most interests them.

Rigid job roles and titles rarely create happy workplaces. As people learn and grow, allowing their job roles to evolve as well is key to keeping them excited and engaged, true partners in co-creating excellence.

MAKE QUALITY CONTAGIOUS

Developing a singular product requires a single-minded focus on quality—whether you are selling rolling papers, coffee, or tubular heating elements. If you're not fanatical about the quality of your product as a founder, you can't expect your customers to be either—or your employees. Unlocking the power of co-creation depends, obviously, on having employees who care.

I got my first glimpse of what it means to truly focus on quality in the factory of my father, an immigrant from Germany. He'd left his home at 12, worked hard, and started a manufacturing company in the Bronx in the 1930s. Still-Man Manufacturing (with "Still-Man" being a combination of his last name and his partner's last name, Altman) made tubular heating elements for appliances, such as steam irons and electric ranges, for the likes of GE and Westinghouse. During World War II, the plant also made parts for weapons.

My father worked seven days a week, and he expected that I'd work hard, too. I started as an employee at his factory the summer when I was 12 years old, the same year that my mother died of cancer. It would probably break child labor laws today, but I got trained to work in the machine shop, where I learned some mechanical drafting and was entrusted with making samples for customers—bending and shaping heating elements to custom specifications.

I enjoyed the work, and seeing my father in his natural environment left an impression. At his company's peak, my father had about 1,000 people working for him; the factory ran 12 shifts a week. The company went public in the early 1960s, and eventually it was sold to Teledyne Technologies, a publicly traded advanced engineering firm. His focus on making a quality product, offering great service, and treating employees well guided me when I started E-Z Wider with my partner, Burt Rubin.

At E-Z Wider, we were obsessive about engineering a product that was objectively better than our competitors'—extra wide, easy to roll, slow burning, with glue that stuck. That meant first traveling across Europe to scout out manufacturers of cellulose-based cigarette papers. US manufacturers only made flax-based paper, which burned faster to achieve lower tar ratings. But pot smokers appreciated the slower burn that cellulose papers provided. We imported big bobbins of paper, about 18 inches in diameter, from European vendors, which we cut, folded, and packaged to our specs in a plant in Manhattan. When we got bigger, we moved to a 30,000-square-foot plant in New Jersey.

Burt and I were constantly trying to fine-tune and improve all aspects of our business—marketing, sales, distribution, customer service, and manufacturing. The knives for cutting paper had to be sharpened and positioned in a particular way. We learned that we needed to "rest" fresh paper bobbins for a few weeks in a climate-controlled room to relax their molecular structure before we cut them. We studied different glues—including strawberry- and banana-flavored—and ways of applying them. We methodically analyzed 40 or 50 variables that we thought could affect the production process. We'd switch operators to see if the operator's skill on the machine was a factor or if the machine itself was producing at a better rate. We kept correcting and perfecting the product itself. We soon realized, for example, that our "wider" paper was a little too wide, so we started selling a 1½-size paper, rather than our original double-wide one. We were also an industry leader in the efficient use of paper.

I strived to bring the same precision and efficiency to the manufacturing of fresh-roasted coffee. But compared with rolling papers, coffee was exponentially more complex. Coffee is an agricultural product, a berrylike fruit that needs to be picked at a certain time and carefully processed. We'd get the green coffee beans in burlap or jute bags shipped from across the globe and delivered directly to our Vermont warehouse by truck. The bags were entered into inventory, and then the beans had to be carefully cleaned.

What's in a bag of green coffee beans, you might ask? We found everything in those sacks from stones, bullets, and teeth to lizards, wedding invitations, and razor blades. Thorough cleaning was a must! The clean coffee would go into a silo until we were ready to roast it as a single-variety coffee or incorporate it into a blend.

Green coffee doesn't resemble coffee as most people know it. It's hard as a rock and has a very musty smell. The enjoyable aroma you get from your coffee comes later with the roasting process. The roasting process also offers plenty of opportunities to ruin good coffee if you're not paying attention. Each variety of coffee has its own taste characteristics that can change dramatically with how you roast it. Unique combinations of soil, climate, and temperature give coffees from Africa, Central America, and Indonesia distinctive regional flavors. But you have variations from lot to lot, too. If one lot of beans from a particular producer is a little bit drier than normal, for example, those beans will roast completely differently—using the same temperature and timing—and produce a different flavor.

To bring out the subtle flavor differences in the beans we were sourcing, we aimed for a medium roast for most of our coffees, which set us apart from the dark and bitter style of roasting that was being popularized on the West Coast, where coffee was often used in drinks that contained a lot of milk. In our first half decade or so, we relied heavily on the same kind of roaster they used in the original Green Mountain store in Waitsfield: a Sivetz fluid-bed roaster. Invented by engineer and coffee lover Michael Sivetz in the 1970s, the contraption used a blower mechanism to float and heat the beans in a column of heated air, like a hot-air popcorn maker. It became popular with specialty coffee roasters because it worked with smaller batches of beans and was relatively affordable. Although it didn't allow the same precision control over roasting as the expensive, drum-style continuous roasters used by large coffee makers, through trial and error, we were able to attain pretty consistent roasting profiles that brought out the best in the arabica beans we were sourcing.

Similar to the extreme focus on details we had at E-Z Wider, we were continually upgrading equipment and examining our processes, aiming for consistency and freshness at a scale few specialty roasters were attempting. But perfection was always a moving target. Many Green Mountain employees can remember me in meetings reciting my mantra: "Better and better," the positive affirmation that I had picked up from reading Émile Coué (first mentioned in Chapter 1), the French pioneer in what's come to be called "positive psychology." For me, repeating the phrase was a way of programming my mind for success. Apparently, though, to some of my employees, it could come across as "Bob is never satisfied!" Dan Cox recalls, "'Better and better' drove everyone crazy after a while, but Bob was really consistent."

Figuring out how we got better and better as a company was something that I saw as everybody's job. It wasn't my responsibility alone. I saw my role as providing a strategy and motivation, not prescribing specific solutions. I wanted people who were close to the work to figure out how to do it better. I wanted the delivery driver to decide the best routes and schedules, the people working the machines to figure out how to make our production line more efficient. I wanted people to think for themselves—not just tell me what I wanted to hear. So I worked strenuously to avoid what I called the "CBS" problem.

I'd learned at some point that certain things were being done CBS, an acronym for "'Cuz Bob says." What was happening was this: As I walked around the company, taking things in and talking with people, one thing or another that I'd asked about or casually mentioned would subsequently be interpreted as an order. I learned about all kinds of things that were supposedly done "'Cuz Bob says" that I'd never said anything explicit about! As a leader in any organization, you need to tread lightly and understand the extra weight that your words can carry. And you need to extend the invitation to collaborate in a clear and consistent way. In the 1980s, this happened informally—by regularly asking employees to think about the work we were doing and to speak honestly about what they felt we could be doing better.

Even without the feedback of employees or other colleagues, one thing I knew we had to commit to was seeking better and better ways of roasting our coffee beans. We quickly outgrew our original roaster in Waitsfield, and in 1982, we set up a factory in the neighboring village of Waterbury. There, we installed a bigger Sivetz roaster—a so-called one-bagger, with a 132-pound capacity—twice that of our roaster in Waitsfield. And we invested in packaging equipment like the big guys were using. We got a weigh-and-fill machine, a new Granulizer (a type of grinder), and a General Packaging Corporation sealer, nicknamed "The General," which allowed us to grind and package coffee in ready-to-brew portions designed for restaurant coffee makers, sealed in foil bags and flushed with nitrogen to keep the contents fresh. These "frac packs" ("frac" stands for fractional) offered a level of convenience for customers that helped justify the higher price of our product. We were also one of the earlier companies to use bags with valves in them that would allow the coffee to de-gas—avoiding the flavor-killing impact of oxidation when beans are left to rest in the open air after roasting.

As we needed more and more equipment—silos for green coffee storage, racks to store roasted coffee, forklifts—just about everything we wanted to buy was a bit bigger than we really needed at the time. But there was nobody making miniature "startup-size" coffee-packaging machines. As a result, we had to "play big" and invest for the company we were going to be tomorrow, not what we were today. This is a common situation for any manufacturing business that needs to put the cart before the horse by acquiring pricey capital assets before it has the sales to justify them. But viewed in a more positive way, it's also a good example of the opportunity mindset in action. Again and again, as our business grew, we needed to overbuild for the future, or we would have ceased to grow at all.

The pace of our investments was, ironically, a red flag for our local bankers. When I started the business, I had developed a relationship with the head of a local bank in Waitsfield. Local banks can be a good place for a small business to get early loans, and I liked being able to walk into the office for a face-to-face meeting. I had gotten a few loans through the bank already—in the $30,000 range for production equipment—and the bank head assured me that as long as we kept meeting our targets, I could keep coming back. We made those targets, and I was hopeful we could continue to borrow. But when we needed to upgrade equipment at the store in Winooski, it was above the credit line our local contact at the bank was allowed to greenlight, and he had to get authorization from his higher-ups. When the bank officers saw the scale of the equipment we were buying, they not only turned us down for a new loan—they also pulled our existing line of credit. They did not have faith in us. I continued to seek lending from local banks, but eventually found that lenders outside the state were more willing to make the larger investments we needed to grow at this point.

As I made the rounds seeking funds for Green Mountain's expansion, I discovered one surefire way to tell if a pitch would succeed, and it didn't require mind reading. Simply put, if the loan officers drank coffee, they would support us. They got it. If they weren't coffee drinkers, almost universally they turned us down. It can make sense to target your fund-raising "asks" to lenders and investors whose interests and experience somehow align with your brand. These kinds of investors, passionate about the product or brand, are also most likely to see themselves not merely as investors, but as partners in co-creating excellence.

SHARE YOUR PASSION FOR THE PRODUCT

Seeking excellence in the coffee we produced, and finding bankers and other investors who would want to work with us, was just part of our challenge. We also had to share positive experiences of our brand if we were going to convince customers to pay more for our ever-improving product. Our retail business was part of that. But we couldn't just wait for people to come into one of our handful of stores. We had to bring the taste of better coffee to them, wherever they were. Without any sort of budget for traditional marketing, we relied on a tried-and-true tool in the marketer's playbook: free samples.

Creating opportunities for people to experience things directly—whether customers or employees—has always been a hallmark of my management style. And in a more digital world, connecting on a physical, experiential level is more important than ever. In-person interactions allow you to share your organization's values and culture and to show what you care about. And the feedback from consumers can reinvigorate your company's collective pursuit of excellence, helping your team come together to set, pursue, and achieve your goals with diligence and enthusiasm.

Food and beverage and consumer packaged goods companies are particularly well suited to in-person sampling, as the cost of goods tends to be low. Stacy's Pita Chips' flagship product began as a giveaway for customers waiting in line for pita sandwiches at Stacy Madison's food cart, but she soon discovered that people would happily pay for them.[4] Red Bull built buzz for a new beverage category by hiring "Red Bull Girls" to hand out energy drinks where young men gathered—at college campuses, bars, and concerts.[5] The free-demo strategy works virtually, too: The "freemium" model has become a staple of tech industry go-to-market strategy, while direct-to-consumer brands have used a sample strategy to lower the barrier to entry in new product/service categories. Most manufacturers are far removed from the customers who actually buy their products. By sharing experiences with potential customers directly—giving them something to try—you have the potential not only to generate goodwill, but to get real-time feedback, too,

We never had Green Mountain Girls, but in the late 1980s, we did have the Coffee Buster—a guy with a big personality who had started selling coffee to people in cars waiting in line at toll booths in the Boston area. The movie *Ghostbusters II* had recently come out, and he dressed up like one of the characters from the movie, in a khaki jumpsuit and a five-gallon insulated container of coffee strapped to his back like a proton pack. One of our sales reps discovered him out there, and we hired him to give away coffee at events throughout New England, with Green Mountain stickers covering his coffee pack. We also gave away tanker trucks worth of coffee to churches and synagogues, which served coffee after services, and to fire stations, police departments, and Kiwanis and Rotary Clubs—all organizations that supported the community. United Way chapters were always important, too; they often had businesspeople associated with them who were potential buyers on our wholesale side.

Soon, we had more employees whose main job was giving away coffee. And the giveaways helped to telegraph our values in a tangible way. Our people were constantly out in the community—offering samples and donations of coffee—and Green Mountain earned a reputation for being generous, as well as a good place to work.

When we did sampling, we had a specific way we wanted people to experience our fine arabica beans, to taste how our roasting process brought out the subtle differences between coffees from Tanzania, Costa Rica, and Sumatra. When we set up a tasting outside one of our stores or at a concert or festival, we'd pour the coffee into little four-ounce paper cups. The cups were too small to add any milk or cream to—and we didn't offer any sugar. We wanted people to taste the coffee on its own.

It was equally important to educate employees about what made our coffee special, so that they tasted the difference, too. At quarterly meetings, our coffee department offered samples of new varieties and explained their origins and unique characteristics. Green Mountain employees were all entitled to take home a pound of coffee every week to enjoy and share with others. I thought this was a no-brainer—and many best-in-class companies do the same: Employees at Ben & Jerry's, for example, can take home up to three free pints of ice cream per day.[6] Workers at New Belgium Brewing Company are entitled to a 12-pack of beer each week. When Green Mountain got bigger, we started a formal program called Java University, offering hands-on training that covered the entire tree-to-cup journey of our product—from growing and harvesting; to roasting and packaging; to grinding, filtering, and brewing. If our employees weren't passionate about our product and our company brand, how could they get other people excited about us?

WIN OVER THE GATEKEEPERS

In addition to embracing and cultivating consumers, investors, and our own employees, we also strived to win over the gatekeepers—distributors, wholesale buyers, and other intermediaries—who are generally the ones who get to decide what consumers can see, use, and taste. In our early years, we were particularly focused on engaging with gatekeepers in the restaurant and hospitality space. In many cases, they were less open to change than consumers were. Educating them required persistence, flexibility, and a thick skin.

Dan Cox was a charming, top-notch salesperson, and he took to the task with a vengeance. He worked for years, for example, to get the

Culinary Institute of America, in Hyde Park, New York, as a customer. This was a big deal. We had all the culinary schools in the country on our prospect list; we wanted to share a better coffee experience with people who were starting careers in the restaurant industry—and the people teaching them. But we had to fight against entrenched tastes. The CIA, as it is known, was one of the top culinary schools in the country; and at the time, in the early 1980s, it ran four restaurants, including the Escoffier Room, one of the highest-rated French restaurants in the country. The school's restaurants served pretty terrible coffee, prepared in funky, outdated equipment. What's more, the curriculum—which offered tons of courses on preparing meat, poultry, fish, and eggs—didn't teach future chefs about coffee.

The chef-instructors at the CIA, we found out, just didn't know the difference between good and bad coffee. In a blind tasting that Dan arranged for them, three out of five chefs preferred Maxwell House over a cup of good, fresh-roasted Colombian coffee. "You're wrong," Dan explained, going on to argue that whatever the chefs themselves preferred, consumer trends were moving toward higher-quality coffee. He explained, nicely, that the chefs just hadn't learned how to evaluate coffee properly. And then he taught them how.

Dan also pulled strings to update their coffee-making equipment, calling up "Hy" Bunn, the CEO of Bunn-O-Matic, and cajoling him into donating about $20,000 worth of equipment to the culinary school. By calling in another favor, he arranged for the Escoffier Room to obtain a fancy new espresso machine. That really endeared us to the folks at the CIA. Not only did they make us their coffee supplier; they also contracted with us to design a coffee-training curriculum for them.

The relationship with the CIA is a great example of co-creating excellence with a customer, and it demonstrates another Better and Better Blueprint principle, too: valuing all stakeholders. We wanted success to accrue across our value chain. By focusing on the success of customers like the CIA, we guaranteed our own. Green Mountain became a long-term trusted partner, rather than just another vendor.

BE GENEROUS WITH KNOWLEDGE

Developing trusted relationships with all your organization's stake-holders also means sharing your knowledge with them in a thoughtful, collegial, and compassionate way. I wanted Green Mountain Coffee to play a role in establishing the specialty coffee industry among the broader public, and I thought the best way to do so would be to share our expertise as widely as possible with consumers—and with our industry peers.

Participating in the emerging specialty coffee industry commu-nity, we shared what we were learning as we went along and benefited immeasurably from the knowledge that others shared with us. While some of us could technically be seen as each other's competitors, I think most of us in the industry saw other coffee companies more as partners on a journey, figuring out together how to get better and to be more successful.

Green Mountain was one of the main supporters of the Specialty Coffee Association of America (now called the Specialty Coffee Association), a trade group founded in 1982. Both Dan Cox and Rick Peyser—who moved from his original job in mail order to manage public relations and eventually became our director of social advocacy and coffee community outreach—served as organization presidents. Each year, Green Mountain would send 20 or 30 people to the SCAA conference. Mike Pelchar, then our national service manager, led packed sessions where he taught brewing techniques. He was really good at it. Other employees would give presentations on roasting technology, coffee sourcing, or other aspects of the business.

Presenting at SCAA and other events helped enhance our pro-file among industry peers, of course. It also gave our employees the positive experience of being recognized by industry peers as "experts," boosting their self-confidence and their overall sense of engagement with the company—both prerequisites for successful co-creation for a higher purpose. Studies of the so-called Pygmalion effect consistently demonstrate the power of positive expectations to impact a person's sense of self, behavior, and performance. Putting employees forward as the face of the company was a powerful way of showing that we believed in them.

There was a genuine camaraderie in the early specialty coffee industry. Everybody wanted to help each other—and I was hungry to learn and to see how we measured up to peers. I remember how Donald Schoenholt, a pioneer in specialty coffee at Gillies Coffee Company in Brooklyn, let me hang out in his store until two in the morning to share ideas about building and running a successful coffee business. We were probably sipping some coffee, too, I imagine!

Visiting George Howell at the Boston-based Coffee Connection (acquired by Starbucks in 1994), I was struck by seeing an entire palette of boxes that he had going out for mail order. And he was sending out one of these once or twice a week! I just kept thinking, "Oh my God, look at all that coffee." In that moment, I saw what I wanted to achieve. Looking back just a few years later, though, that was nothing! By then, we were shipping out whole tractor-trailer loads. But having that image as a specific vision to aim for was tremendously motivating.

The network of specialty coffee producers would also be instrumental in promoting industry standards and philanthropic efforts to help coffee-growing communities. Coffee Kids was founded in 1988 by Bill Fishbein, who started the Coffee Exchange in Providence, Rhode Island. It was one of the first independent nonprofits to focus on improving prospects for young coffee farmers. Originally, because Coffee Exchange was a competitor, I remember thinking, "Should we really support this?" But I felt we had both an obligation to help these coffee farmers and an opportunity to improve coffee quality and help the industry. Green Mountain was a company committed to a higher purpose, to using our business as a force for good. Whether we did that on our own, or in partnership with others, was less important than simply trying to do the right thing. For years, Green Mountain employees served on the Coffee Kids board and in various leadership roles including president. When we later expanded our own philanthropic programs in coffee-growing communities, our Central America connections through Coffee Kids proved invaluable.

PUT YOUR PEOPLE FIRST

"Getting things done"—roasting the coffee, selling it, and delivering it—was the driving force in building our company culture in the beginning. In our journey to co-create excellence, there was always something to do. If you weren't already busy on a Saturday or a holiday night, it was understood that you'd pitch in at the warehouse helping to pack coffee. While this is a well-known part of working at a startup company, it's important for leaders to make sure that a sense of commitment on employees' part doesn't lead to burnout. One way I tried to prevent this was by hiring enough people to actually do the work and budgeting extra time for training and development—too many employers knowingly run short-staffed in order to trim expenses, which leads to declines in quality and morale. We also made sure that people took the time off they were entitled to.

But when it came to working, and working hard, we were definitely an "all-hands-on-deck" organization, where everyone chipped in to help one another. It seems as though we always needed someone to make deliveries! And we were always dealing with surprises—like getting our first tractor-trailer load of coffee delivered in the mid-1980s. We hadn't yet built a real loading dock at our roasting facility in Waterbury, and nobody had given much thought to how exactly we'd unload this giant truckload of coffee.

The raw beans came in sacks, which were piled on the floor of the truck rather than stacked on palettes, to avoid tearing the material. We had the truck pull up to a garage door with a high bay and got two people in the truck to start loading bags onto dollies. They'd wheel these to the back of the truck, where a couple of more folks would load them onto a palette and then someone would drive them into the warehouse with a forklift. It took 5½ hours to unload a single truck that way. We were always on the lookout for ways to improve processes and help employees with their jobs, though—and after the purchase of a machine called a "strong-arm manipulator," we were able to do the same job with two people in about 45 minutes.

We experienced all sorts of growing pains, of course. For some reason, we always seemed to screw up the first delivery to a new whole-sale account. We'd have meetings and talk about ways to improve, but to my dismay, it became part of the company culture—an inside joke. I'd hoped that we would get it right for our first delivery to IBM in the mid-1980s. IBM had a chip-making plant outside Burlington that employed thousands of people—a very big account for us. But true to form, we messed up, accidentally double-billing them on a $3,000 order. To our surprise, the company simply paid it. But we pointed out our error, of course, and put even more effort into serving IBM's account going forward. We got really good at fixing our mistakes, though, and we used to joke that it was part of our brand building—screwing things up just to show how good we were at making them right.

I screwed up, too, and sometimes failed to show enough appreciation, personally, for the hard work employees were putting in. One hot summer night, I was working late and ran into Mike Pelchar, who'd just gotten back from driving an exhausting delivery route in an extended Ford van with nonfunctioning air conditioning. As I left my office and walked to my car, I went over to Mike and thanked him "for going above and beyond." I'm not sure what I was expecting, but Mike was hot and a bit irritable. "That's good to know," he said. "But I'm not the only one around here that goes above and beyond. And if you really wanted to thank me, you would buy me a beer someday after work."

I slunk into my car and drove off. Mike was right. When I saw him working late again as I left the office the following week, I pulled over and rolled down my window. "Can I buy you a beer?" I asked. He laughed and got in. It's so important to remember that money is nice, but appreciation takes other, more important forms, too.

As we struggled and stumbled along, I made a point of celebrating our wins, both inside the company and beyond, embracing a principle that would later become a central part of the Better and Better Blueprint. Every time we got a new account, we'd send a note out, and employees would make a point to stop in at the business and thank the people there in person. It was important to me that employees realize how all their personal interactions on behalf of Green Mountain were part of our marketing and public relations. In turn, I believe that employees seeing themselves as representatives of the company boosted their pride and self-esteem. How they spoke, behaved, dressed—these were a reflection on the organization. Dan Cox recalls how, in 1983, we started to make some headway commercially and got some official Green Mountain apparel—polos and button-down shirts with logos for the sales group. "We were really proud to wear that," Dan says. The delivery of our first custom-painted delivery van soon after was a celebratory turning point, visible evidence that we were here to stay.

By the end of the 1980s, we were well known in our community and were growing players in the specialty coffee industry. Personally, I had settled in, too. My wife, Christine, and our two children, Jules and David, had moved into a comfortable house in Shelburne, Vermont. My son Christian was soon born there in 1988. Green Mountain had become, if not exactly a well-oiled machine, an extremely resilient and cohesive group. I could now see that our main competitive advantage was our ability to work together as a team. And perhaps nothing better illustrates the way that employees take charge when they have a sense of ownership than the way our company responded to what became known, in company lore, as the "Big Bang."

One summer morning in the late 1980s as I pulled up to the plant around 10 o'clock, an employee named Carol Gysek, who worked in our roasting operation, came running outside and started banging on my window. The workers inside were desperately trying to put out a fire. Carol breathlessly explained that they'd put a load of green coffee beans into the big Sivetz roaster, and the machine had stalled. So rather than floating on a bed of hot air, the coffee beans had stopped moving and dropped down to the 500-degree-plus surface on the bottom of the machine. The operators did the right thing by shutting the machine off right away. But instead of carefully pulling the smoldering beans out with a scraper, they decided to open up a chute at one end of the machine and blast the fan to push them out one side. The sudden rush of oxygen into the smoking chamber caused a massive explosion that blew the top right off the whole machine like a volcano.

Two employees had to be taken to the hospital, but luckily no one was seriously hurt. The fire department arrived to put out the fire, but unfortunately ruined our expensive equipment in the process. (Later, we'd give the employees a much better education about how to handle similar fires in ways less destructive to our investments—and implement a ton of new cleaning and safety procedures!)

After almost a decade in business, we were finally getting some real momentum. We'd recently gotten our first big supermarket account on board. But now, with our primary roaster down, we couldn't make coffee for the customer. Paul Comey, still working as a consultant, quickly identified and ordered a new roaster, an upgrade on the Sivetz called the Probat EN500. But the machine had to ship from Germany and would take a month or so to reach us. Shutting down in the meantime was not an option—and everyone in the company, now 100 people or so, seemed to realize that. We sprang into action.

We shifted as much additional roasting as we could into our stores, and had employees picking up fresh-roasted beans throughout the day and bringing them back to our distribution center. But the in-store roasters could do only about 30 pounds at a time—hardly commercial scale. So we called up one of our friends from the SCAA, at River Road Coffee in Malone, New York, a 2½-hour drive away on bad country roads through the Adirondacks. At least twice a week after that, someone—often our long-suffering plant manager Curtis Hooper, whose big, deep laugh belied the pressure he was always under—would load up a 32-foot truck with green coffee beans in 55-gallon metal drums, drop them off in Malone, and return with the previous batch that River Road Coffee had roasted for us.

That was a very long month. And when the new roaster arrived, its advanced blower system required the installation of extensive new ductwork. You couldn't just plug it in where the old one was. But the manufacturer said it never saw an installation go so quickly. And less than two months after the Big Bang, we were up and running again with increased capacity, more inspired and unified than ever.

There was no longer any question about whether we were engaged in co-creating excellence, and there was no longer any question about whether we would make it. The question was how fast we could grow.

LESSONS TO GO

Focus relentlessly on product quality. If you and your employees aren't obsessed with what you're making, you can't expect a customer to be.

Cultivate consumers through education. There is a learning curve with any innovative product or service. Invest the time you need to teach consumers why you're worth it.

Make sure that all employees understand and appreciate your core product or service. Think "tree to cup." Explain the A-to-Z process that imbues your core products and services with value. Don't assume that someone in IT or HR doesn't care about how the coffee is made.

Share experiences that showcase your organization and your products or other offerings in a positive light. For instance, free samples and product donations are low-cost ways to generate buzz and foster a connection with potential customers, while gathering direct feedback you can use to improve.

Share knowledge. Position your employees as industry experts— and help them build self-confidence—by encouraging them to attend and present at conferences and other industry events. If you're in a new industry, a strategy of helping others to succeed can help you gain recognition as a thought leader.

Hire for mindset over skill set. Expertise is often overrated. Focus instead on the importance of a positive attitude, on people's ability to work well with one another in co-creating excellence, and on how well they fit with your company culture.

Put people first. Say thanks. Show appreciation personally. Valuing all stakeholders starts with valuing your employees, and rewarding them for living up to company values will reinforce those values.

3

THE GAS STATION COFFEE

Winning with a Focus on Customer Success

••

I n December 1991, ten years following our launch, we were featured for the first time in *Forbes*. The article "Hippie Redux" noted our seven retail stores in the Northeastern United States, our 1,000-plus restaurant and gourmet food store accounts—and our slim $200,000 net profit on total sales of about $11 million.[1] Americans' taste in coffee was changing, and our growing sales proved it. But even though we were selling coffee at a rate equivalent to 1 million cups per day, we were still just a regional brand barely breaking even. Starbucks and other coffee concepts were growing quickly. To remain competitive, we needed to be growing much faster.

I had recently turned down an acquisition offer from a New York City investor who was building a network of specialty coffee companies and had acquired several of our competitors. So we had to find capital elsewhere. My bank lenders didn't have an appetite for the big investments we needed, and at that time, venture capital wasn't really an option for a company like ours. Instead, we went public, with an initial public offering on the Nasdaq Small Cap exchange in September 1993. Today, no company as small as we were then—with sales of about $15 million a year—would do an IPO except out of desperation. But it was the way to move forward. The $11.5 million we raised in the stock offering let us hire a few more seasoned people, open new stores, invest in mail-order catalogs, and buy new packaging machinery that extended the shelf life of coffee sold in supermarkets.

I saw all these things as foundational for future growth. I was still convinced that combining wholesale and retail models was key to maximizing coffee consumption in one geographic area after another—ensuring that our product was available in every channel where a consumer might seek it. As in our retail stores, we sought to bring wholesale customers into the culture of Green Mountain by giving them an experience of something better than they were accustomed to. This applied not only to our core product—fresh-roasted coffee of the highest quality—but to every aspect of service, as well. Appreciating the unique challenges of customers in diverse market channels, we distinguished ourselves from competitors with tailored point-of-sale solutions, creative merchandising, and next-level teamwork. We became partners in our customers' success, treating them as valued stakeholders in our own business.

Embracing our core values of collaboration, empathy, and helpfulness, we realized Green Mountain's potential in ways that even I couldn't have imagined—and came to better appreciate where our strengths lay as an organization. By leaning into our wholesale business, from 1994 to 1996, we turned a loss of nearly $3 million into net income of nearly $2 million, and by 1997 our net sales had nearly doubled. This chapter illustrates the synergy and exponential business growth that was created across our wholesale business by valuing all our company's stakeholders—in the first instance by helping promote our customers' success in retailing our coffee products. Of course, a company's stakeholders generally include not only its customers, but also, among others, its employees, suppliers, shareholders, and the communities where it makes and/or markets its products. Across the pages of this book, I'll try to impart just how important it is to strive to appreciate the perspectives and fulfill the needs and desires of all these groups.

CREATE TAILORED EXPERIENCES THAT PROMOTE CUSTOMER SUCCESS (AND SHOW YOUR BRAND AT ITS BEST)

As I mapped out the wholesale market for our coffee in the early 1990s, I saw endless opportunities to get our brand in front of consumers. I wanted Green Mountain to be the unexpectedly fresh coffee you got on the train, on the plane, at the ski lodge, in the college dining hall, at the gas station convenience store, and at the supermarket.

Green Mountain's wholesale strategy was to identify underserved but monetarily significant niches of the coffee market and "flood" them—offering a level of service and support that would set us apart. We tried to surprise and delight our wholesale customers with targeted point-of-sale solutions that solved their problems and boosted their profits, even as they promoted our brand.

People drink a lot of coffee in the office, and more importantly, the office is where many people can develop a coffee-drinking "habit." If we could win people over to our brand at work, they would buy our coffee at the supermarket and elsewhere. And so we worked diligently to enter the office coffee service business, working with distributors and, later, office-supply retailers. Once we identified an opportunity, we spared no effort to connect the dots and to make our customers—and therefore our company—successful. Through a breakthrough deal with Staples and Poland Spring in 1997, we expanded our distribution into thousands of offices across the Northeast United States. And to further our relationships in the channel, we developed a gift catalog for businesses, with volume discounts so they could recognize their clients, vendors, and friends.

We worked hard to get into the college market, too. After all, if you can develop a relationship with students while they are in college, you can win lifelong consumers. The college market was very much in tune with our emerging work around organic and Fair Trade coffees, which gave us a competitive advantage in bidding against many traditional institutional coffee providers. Students at universities across New England—including young people at Amherst College, Babson College, the University of Vermont, and the University of New Hampshire—were fueled by Green Mountain Coffee.

Our strategy, again, was to be *everywhere* coffee was sold and to forge a positive experience of the Green Mountain brand. The transportation sector offered yet further opportunities to deliver a better coffee experience in an unexpected place. To score Amtrak as a customer, we had to develop a special machine for serving coffee on the trains. A basic metal box, more functional than pretty, it had some complex engineering inside, allowing it to operate intermittently and to flush out all the water between batches of coffee. This was because sometimes the trains would lose power, and if the coffee maker froze with water inside, the ice would break the machine. We also got Green Mountain Coffee served in the waiting areas and lounges for Delta Express flights in Boston and other airports across the Northeast. We didn't get our coffee on the planes themselves, but that was probably for the best—issues with the purity of airplane water made it challenging to serve coffee that could meet our quality standards.

We made inroads in hospitality and food service—with accounts including Aureole, a Michelin-starred restaurant in New York, now closed; the Culinary Institute of America (mentioned earlier in Chapter 2); and the Harvard Club—and in the recreation and retail sectors. By the late 1990s, our customers included the American Skiing Company, which operated nine resorts across the Northeast and had more than 5 million customer visits per year; 80-plus Hoyts Cinemas locations; WeightWatchers, which offered Green Mountain coffee at its meetings; and L.L. Bean, which supplied coffee at its flagship store in Freeport, Maine, and sold bagged coffee through its catalog. These were all lucrative opportunities that were out there. Anybody could have pursued them. But it required an opportunity mindset to recognize them and to focus our collective efforts into making customers in these channels successful.

· · · · · · ·

In 1986, Dan Cox came to me with the exciting news that we'd landed our first multimillion-dollar supermarket account—with Kings, a 21-store chain in New Jersey—which had come about because the CEO had visited our store in Portland, Maine, while on vacation. Dan had acted quickly to seal the deal.

But now that we'd gotten the account, I asked Dan, "How are we going to keep them?" Supermarkets were always central to my long-term strategy, as more pounds of coffee were sold in this channel for home consumption than anywhere else. When the opportunity with Kings came up, we had no retail presence or distribution infrastructure in New Jersey. But it was an incredible opportunity. We just had to work hard—and move fast—to meet the company's demanding specs, and at the same time create a compelling in-store experience of our brand.

We sold both prepackaged whole beans and bulk beans that were sold by weight. For bulk coffee, we needed to create our own displays—the idea was to have the whole beans in clear bins, and customers could scoop, bag, and grind the coffee themselves. Since there was no one who made these displays at the time, we had to find a Lucite supplier and design and build them ourselves, hiring a 19-year-old named Jason King to lead the project. We certainly weren't going to let the opportunity slip by because we didn't have the right displays!

Next to the bulk coffee bins, we supplied and serviced coffee grinders for customers to use—one for regular coffee, one for flavored. People were always screwing up, of course, and putting flavored coffee in the nonflavored coffee grinder. Or they left ground coffee in the machine, so that when the next customer opened the gate, it all spilled out onto the floor. We made sure to maintain good relationships with the supermarket staff responsible for those areas, and they would go out of their way to help address problems. Eventually, we employed a team of stockers to ensure that supermarket displays were clean, appropriately stocked, and well promoted. Most of our competitors in the wholesale segment did not provide such high levels of support.

The extra effort spent on merchandising was well worth it for the visceral coffee experience we provided—a supermarket version of the original Green Mountain Coffee Roasters café experience. For customers who had grown up with coffee from a can, it was a novelty to be able to grind whole beans and enjoy their intoxicating smell. It was a way for us to share an unexpected positive experience of our brand in the supermarket aisle—while helping the supermarkets to differentiate themselves from their competitors.

As part of our effort to make sure that early supermarket customers were successful in retailing our coffee, Dan Cox had the idea of guiding their shoppers to the Green Mountain Coffee Roasters area with eye-catching, specially designed faux-wood Green Mountain signs. Dan hand-painted the first batch of 10 signs himself. Soon, we placed a second order for 30 more.

We had to modify our pricing model for supermarkets, too, adjusting to their "line pricing" policies. What this meant was that all coffee sold in bulk as whole beans had to be uniformly priced, at, say, $8.99 a pound. The supermarket buyers didn't care about our raw material costs. We just had to make it work. It's what the customer needed.

By showing how hard we were willing to work to create successful outcomes, we grew our footprint rapidly. By 1999, we were selling into more than 570 supermarkets throughout the Northeast. My vision of a virtuous cycle—where consumers who encountered Green Mountain at the office, at school, or on a road trip could be sure to find it at the supermarket, too—was becoming real.

TAKE THE HIGHWAY LESS TRAVELED

New distribution channels come with risks, of course, and as we expanded our wholesale business, we had to be mindful of trade-offs between brand exposure and reputational risk. If you're selling a premium product, you don't typically want to be associated with a nonpremium channel. To be sure, there was nothing glamorous about gas station convenience stores—and they were an unlikely showcase for high-quality specialty coffee. It took an ever-keen opportunity mindset to appreciate the potential for transformation there. But we did, and by following the same approach we took across our wholesale business—valuing customers as stakeholders, co-creating solutions to help their businesses grow, and committing to the highest level of quality and service—we transformed it into a remarkable success, becoming the most widely distributed "gas station coffee" in the country.

It all started with a single ExxonMobil gas station account in Maine in 1990. The store was across from a Dunkin' Donuts, and the owner was resigned to being outcompeted on the coffee front. But our rep up in Maine convinced the owner to take a chance on Green

Mountain. He came to believe that we could make his store more suc-cessful. And we did. His coffee sales increased fivefold, and because he owned several other stores, they, too, switched to Green Mountain and saw similar outcomes. Soon, word started flowing through the network of ExxonMobil's franchisees in the Northeast and then nationally. By 1996, we were in over 800 stores in 17 states.

From the get-go, I faced pushback about bringing the Green Mountain brand into these no-frills stores. Dan Cox, who had worked hard to win prestige accounts like the Culinary Institute and the Harvard Club, worried that these legacy customers wouldn't take well to seeing their "gourmet" coffee sitting across the aisle from the chips and the Slim Jim meat sticks. As we considered expanding within the ExxonMobil network, I remember a board member who had come from Nestlé Canada framing the strategic question rather memorably: "Why would you want to be associated with shitty gas station cof-fee?" He brought it up at several board meetings. Then he happened to stay at a high-end bed-and-breakfast that served Green Mountain Coffee—and found out the folks at the B&B were serving it because they'd discovered it at a gas station convenience store down the road from them. He finally got it.

Almost everybody, from all economic walks of life, goes to the gas station—and probably far more often than they go to a nice res-taurant. It was true that no one expected to find good coffee in a gas station. Why couldn't we change that and promote our brand up and down the roadways of America? At this stage in our business—as long as we presented our brand with quality, freshness, and care—I didn't see it as a huge risk. The way we could avoid being associated with "shitty gas station coffee" was to make sure we avoided serving that kind of inferior product.

Back then, in gas station convenience stores, the dominant cof-fee "delivery system"—a glass pot sitting on a burner for hours—was less than ideal. Even if the first cups of freshly brewed coffee poured from that pot might have been fine, after a half hour, the coffee would taste tired and burnt. We were always seeking out new technol-ogy that could help us produce, package, and serve better and better coffee—and I didn't care whether we invented it or someone else did, as long as it improved the coffee experience. Fortunately, in light of our growing reputation in the industry, people would often come to us with new ideas and new technologies. Steve Sabol, who in the early 1990s worked in product development, was the gatekeeper of all these innovations. In 1990 or so, he came to me with a new kind of insulated container he'd spotted at a Specialty Coffee Association conference, an early air pot.

By now, everyone has seen these big silver contraptions. But at the time, air pots—insulated containers with a pump mechanism on top—were a total game changer for ensuring fresh hot coffee. They eliminated the problem of how to keep coffee warm without burning it, and they were quick and simple to use. That said, as early adopters, we still experienced the sort of problems that inevitably arise with any new technology. Early models had a glass liner and were prone to breaking, which meant sometimes the pots had to be repaired or entirely replaced. But the improvement in coffee quality was worth it. Better to be early, I thought. And an updated version of those first air pots remains one of the most common ways you'll find coffee served in any gas station convenience store today.

As much as I worried about keeping pace with innovations to maintain the quality of the coffee we served at convenience stores, I also wanted to make sure we remained nimble and effective in our in-store marketing of our products. Gas stations and convenience stores were familiar territory to me from my E-Z Wider days, and I approached the in-store merchandising of our coffee in these stores in a way that was not so different from what I'd done with rolling papers—creating distinctive signage and offering merchandise that promoted our brand and delivered extra revenue opportunities for store owners. Our distinctive faux-carved wood Green Mountain sign became a road-trip beacon, hanging beneath the Exxon or Mobil sign. (They were also frequently stolen.) I learned about one moving company that went back and forth between Vermont and Maine and shared locations of all the gas stations that served Green Mountain Coffee—those were the only places the drivers wanted to stop!

We also developed a reusable plastic travel mug—bright orange with our logo on it—and gas station convenience stores sold tens of thousands of them. We made and sold these as cheaply as possible—we didn't care about making money on them. They were a way to keep our brand in front of customers, and by cutting down on the use of Styrofoam cups, we were doing our part to help the environment. We'd go on to make a range of reusable mugs—celebrating company anniversaries or awards we'd received. To this day, I still have the mug celebrating an award we received from Jane Goodall after working with her on a coffee line to support her work with chimpanzees in Tanzania. I remember another mug with the slogan "Sip and Relax," echoing an ad campaign we were running: "Sip and relax, you're on Green Mountain time." The hope was to heighten the experience of the coffee by making people more mindful. At a time when Styrofoam cups were still the norm, providing customers with an eye-catching reusable mug allowed them to express their principles—and to promote ours, too. Those Green Mountain mugs traveled far and wide!

Our marketing innovations soon extended to codeveloping store designs, too. As a trusted ExxonMobil partner, we were brought in to help develop the company's "On the Run" store concept, which was being prototyped in a secret warehouse. This is a great example of what I would later define as the Better and Better Blueprint principle of co-creating excellence, in this case with a customer. By 2000, ExxonMobil would be our biggest single customer, accounting for about 18 percent of sales. And in November of that year, we beat out 11 rival companies to sign a five-year contract to supply 1,200 ExxonMobil gas station convenience stores, plus an additional 500 corporate-owned stores; and we became the preferred provider for the company's 14,000 dealer and franchise operators, as well as for their corporate offices.

The real-world brand impressions we created in gas station convenience stores did more for us than traditional advertising and marketing ever could have. Getting consumers to buy something new is hard—recent research from Nielsen, for example, found that in the US consumer packaged goods market, just 4.3 percent of consumers' brick-and-mortar purchases involve a brand they have not purchased before. We saw our growing convenience store presence translate into sales in the supermarket channel, too. In 2001, Green Mountain coffee could be found in over 1,050 chain supermarket locations. And more than three-quarters of all the coffee we sold, by the pound, was in just three channels: convenience stores (29.1 percent), offices (24.4 percent), and supermarkets (24 percent). This was a remarkable testament to the transformation we'd undergone in the past decade—and showed us clearly where our strengths lay. We made great coffee, but probably just as important, we were doing a great job of helping our customers sell it.

EXECUTION IS A COMPETITIVE EDGE

While initially my strategy for Green Mountain's wholesale coffee business involved creating solutions for underserved market channels, our success in these channels eventually caught the attention of competitors. That didn't worry me too much, though. Competitors could try to match the quality of our products or develop similar service offerings in specific market channels. But I was confident that no one could do a better job taking care of customers than we did.

Former Zappos CEO Tony Hsieh talked about his business as a customer service company that just happened to sell shoes.[2] We thought about our wholesale business in a similar way. We put a focused effort on keeping our wholesale customers happy, working together to make them more successful, demonstrating the Better and Better Blueprint principle of valuing *all* our stakeholders. We invested considerable time and resources in really understanding what customers needed from us as a vendor, and developing or improving systems and processes to support them as personally and consistently as possible.

In the mid-1990s, I became very interested in formally defining core processes in our business, establishing metrics for improvement, and working with IT and cross-departmental teams to optimize our performance. A "process" is simply a series of tasks and actions that lead to a particular business result. Our "Order to Cash" process, for example, consisted of the series of actions that go from taking a customer order, to packing and delivering the order, to collecting the money to pay for it.

Our senior leadership team defined about a half dozen business processes and created cross-functional teams made up of representatives from all the groups involved in the process. These teams worked on figuring out how to make their processes either more efficient, more cost-effective, or easier and quicker to complete—or all three. In addition to Order to Cash, these processes included Procure to Pay (getting the materials and resources we needed and paying for them), Market to Sell (self-explanatory), New Products and Promotions (internal processes to create and implement), and Plan to Produce (planning and producing completed coffee products). Another process worked on reducing the time it took to close our monthly financial statements, which involved getting information from all the departments in a form that was easily translated into the information needed. People enjoyed being on these teams and making a contribution to improving our effectiveness.

Embracing new technologies was key to enabling these process-innovation efforts. From the beginning, Green Mountain was a more high-tech company than most of our competitors, with my specific interest in computers going back to an early job as a systems analyst at Columbia University in the late 1960s. (At the time, the university was still using punch cards for some of its operations!) I always believed that embracing new technologies would give Green Mountain a competitive advantage, and I aimed to integrate IT into the business starting in the 1980s, investing in systems and hiring tech experts to keep us on the cutting edge. To work with large customers like grocery chains, in the early 1990s, we adopted electronic data interchange, a system that allows trading partners to send information to another company electronically in a standardized format. We launched an inventory-management database and adopted bar coding to gain more real-time awareness of what was moving in and out of our warehouses. In 1993, with 2,400 wholesale accounts and sales of about $15 million, Green Mountain became the launch customer for new state-of-the-art roasting control software developed by a New Jersey company, giving us unprecedented consistency, reducing costs, and improving safety. The same year, we hired a new chief information officer, Jim Prevo, who brought 13 years' experience working at Digital Equipment Corporation, a major US microprocessor manufacturer.

In 1998, we became one of the smallest, if not the smallest, business customers for PeopleSoft supply chain management and CRM software (acquired by Oracle in 2004), at a cost of over $1 million. That was a big software commitment for a company our size, with sales of about $56 million at the time. But like the packaging machines we had to buy that were designed for companies much bigger than ours, IT infrastructure was something we needed now, and investing in it required an opportunity mindset. While it may have been more than we needed when we first invested, the software systems we implemented were essential to our future growth, allowing us to integrate a string of acquired companies in the late 2000s without disrupting the overall organization.

Technology indeed helped us to be better partners with many of our company's most important stakeholders: suppliers, distributors, customers, and our own employees. Within the company, it helped us sustain a highly collaborative approach to account management. Across Green Mountain's wholesale business, the management of accounts was the responsibility of a team that included employees in sales, in delivery and service, and in accounts receivable. Anyone who "touched" the customers would be concerned with taking care of them, with the goal of maximizing their satisfaction and minimizing our losses. It wasn't just accounts receivable that chased down customer invoices, for example—the Order to Cash process that we had developed made everyone in the chain, from sales to delivery, responsible for getting us paid.

We strived to create redundancy so that our customers would be regularly touched by employees from across our company. (Our strategy of building up density of customers in a particular area helped us to do that more efficiently.) As explained above, we provided whole-sale customers with brewing, grinding, and other coffee-making equipment, along with product displays, at no charge. We installed the equipment and repaired it when needed. This provided us with numerous opportunities to interact with our customers—and to make an impression. If a customer was out of coffee, the customer could call the delivery person, but the equipment-service person might drop it off. Or if a delivery person or a sales rep was near a customer that needed help with equipment, there was an expectation that that person would jump in and help fix it. At no point in the process could anyone say, "It's not in my job description."

While many of our competitors eventually started outsourcing these kinds of support services, I wanted to keep everything we could in-house. Even if using third-party vendors was cheaper, I wanted to create a relationship with customers, not just ship coffee to them. Showing up in person is a far more effective way to do that. Initially, our retail stores served as support hubs for wholesale accounts in their area. Eventually, though, I came to appreciate that there was a conflict in this model, because we were essentially asking our own retail stores to support other retailers in their area who were technically their competitors. Instead, we opened warehouses called regional operations centers that would distribute coffee, service equipment, and serve as a home base for salespeople and other support people in that area.

If wholesale customers are key stakeholders in your business, caring for them in innovative ways and giving them personal attention reinforces the value you place on them. And this all-hands approach helped us to pick up on problems and make changes quickly. A delivery person might notice signs of dissatisfaction before a service rep could.

A June 2021 study by Deloitte Digital, "The End of Incrementalism," argues that for top-performing sales organizations, the model of a single primary point of contact for customers is outdated: "As customer expectations continue to rise and personalization at scale becomes the norm, the lines between marketing, sales, service, and product team touchpoints will blur, and the lines between these organizations will blur as well."[3] Software-as-a-service (SaaS) companies have been blurring roles for some time, introducing "customer success" teams that split the difference between sales and service.

Seeing our success in the wholesale coffee business, plenty of competitors copied aspects of what we were doing, including some of the specialized service innovations we brought to our customers. Our competitive advantage was how well we executed—how far we would go to work together and get the job done. It was hard for anyone to copy that, because it emerged authentically from our commitments to co-creating excellence, sharing positive experiences, and valuing all our stakeholders. As much as we were selling a product, coffee, we were selling the experience of working with our people, which is one reason we focused so much on helping them, as individuals and teams, to learn and continuously improve.

CULTIVATE COMMITMENT AT EVERY LEVEL

Everyone who interacts with customers represents your company and values. Knowing that all your colleagues will make you proud in these interactions comes down to culture. With this in mind, we made sure that modeling this kind of helping behavior was part of our company's DNA. Toward that end, I often told my colleagues the story of an employee named Craig. He had gone out to make some deliveries to local customers during a snowstorm, and as it got later and he hadn't come back, everyone started wondering what had happened. When Craig finally showed up, covered in snow, he explained that he'd stopped to pull someone's car out of a ditch. He did that not because he was a Green Mountain employee, but because he was a good human being. But he also knew that going out of his way to do the right thing was always the right business move.

Clearly communicating values and priorities inside your organization is essential to instilling a customer-first approach. The luxury Ritz-Carlton hotel brand explicitly empowers every employee to make things right for guests. In their training, employees learn the company's "Twelve Service Values."[4] Among them: "I own and immediately resolve guest problems," and "I am empowered to create unique, memorable and personal experiences for our guests." At one time, every employee, from housekeeping to management, could spend up to $2,000 per guest, per day, to resolve a guest problem.[5] At Green Mountain, we never put a dollar limit on creating a satisfied customer. But everyone knew to do whatever was needed to fix an account.

As much as they were committed to customers, our employees—and especially our salespeople—were passionate about our product and ensuring that, regardless of sales channel, it was served at its best. That was a way of protecting our brand reputation, of course—if a wholesale customer "screwed up" the last mile of coffee service, it made us look bad. But ultimately, by making sure our coffee was served at its very best, we knew we could in turn help our customers achieve optimal success, too.

In the 1990s, our longtime production manager Curtis Hooper had the job of ensuring that our wholesale accounts were brewing our coffee properly. He was helped by committed deputies like Tom Rutz, one of our top sales reps. As we were working out a deal to increase our footprint in ExxonMobil's convenience-store network, Tom went to meet with some of their bigwigs in Alexandria, Virginia. As part of our expansion in the stores, we wanted them all to switch to air pots—which had dramatically improved the quality of coffee served in stores that were using them—instead of glass carafes. Their top guy in this meeting balked. He liked how the old glass pots looked, and he didn't care when Tom pointed out that with the air pots, you didn't need to rebrew coffee every 20 minutes to maintain freshness.

Finally, Tom couldn't take it anymore. Suddenly, he looked up and said, "Have you even been in your stores? You can't keep the bathrooms clean! How are you going to maintain the coffee?"

The room went silent. The ExxonMobil executive, clearly agitated, reiterated, "We're doing it in glass pots."

"Not with my coffee!" Tom said, standing up to leave.

"Wait a minute!" the ExxonMobil bigwig called after him. "Nobody says that to me. Let's talk about it some more." Tom had shown that he was fanatical about the quality of coffee he was selling, and not surprisingly, he got his way.

You might ask if you really want employees who are willing to walk away like Tom was. Well, I know that serving our coffee in glass pots wouldn't have represented our product well. And as a result, the customer wouldn't have been successful. Given the situation, and the stubbornness of the players involved, Tom's hardball tactics may have been the only way to get that point across. He wasn't saying, "We don't care about what you think." Instead, he was saying, in essence, "We care about your optimal success, and we're not going to let you fall short of achieving it!"

WHAT YOU'RE REALLY SELLING IS SUCCESS

We used to have a "rule" among our sales team that we'd never talk about price until we'd gotten a prospective wholesale customer to sample the coffee. "Who cares what the price is?" we'd say. "Let's *taste* the coffee!" This goes back to my belief in the unmatched power of experience to change perceptions, create empathy, and motivate action. It was also a way to shift the discussion to a more important question, which was not "How much does it cost?" but rather "How much more will we be able to sell?"

In tastings, we always had to beat New England Tea & Coffee and Dunkin' Donuts—the big guys. Pound for pound, our coffee was more expensive than either of theirs. But we knew that our coffee was better. If potential customers could taste that difference—which they usually could—agreeing on terms wouldn't be too hard. (If they couldn't, we would have our work cut out for us!)

Because it tasted better, we pretty much guaranteed that customers would sell more coffee, more than offsetting the premium price. Even the most expensive coffee in the world is cheap by the cup. Our sales team was good at breaking down the math. If our coffee cost 50 cents more by the pound, that comes out to a few cents more per cup. With our coffee, they could charge 5 or 10 cents more a cup and make a considerable profit—or they could keep the price the same and attract more customers, and by selling just one extra cup per pound they could easily cover the cost difference. As we gained more brand recognition, we could also make the case that people would go out of the way to buy our coffee.

By sharing an experience—going through the trouble of doing a real coffee tasting versus just coming in and selling coffee—and laying out our "coffee economics" in a way that was easy for buyers to understand, we got prices that were often significantly higher than our competitors'. And cup by convenience-store cup, those extra cents added up—both for our business and for our customers.

INVITE CUSTOMERS IN

Beyond offering a higher level of service and support than our competitors did, we strove to actively engage wholesale customers in Green Mountain's company culture in real, experiential ways. I believed in the unsurpassed benefits of involving stakeholders—including our customers—in the details of our business, sharing information, knowledge, and appreciation. This goes to my belief in engaging the whole system, valuing and drawing on multiple stakeholder perspectives in setting strategy and co-creating excellence in our products and processes. The way we did this set us apart from competitors and helped us create enthusiastic partnerships that spread the Green Mountain "experience" and the ideas that we valued far and wide.

In the same way we shared information about the company with employees, empowering them to make things better, we shared data with wholesale customers, providing them with sales history, forecasting, merchandising data, and more. In return, they could provide us with valuable feedback on consumer behavior, the effectiveness of merchandising, and other such metrics. We were pioneers in having sales managers use laptop computers in the field, which enabled them to set up new customers more efficiently and to pull up reports on demand, sharing information that helped us compete more effectively.

We also put a lot of focus on customer education. We invited businesses that sold our coffee in their restaurants, hotels, or convenience stores to attend our employee training program, called Coffee College, an intensive two-day course that covered growing and harvesting; roasting and packaging; grinding, filtering, and brewing—everything behind the perfect cup of coffee. Usually, this meant inviting them to our Waterbury, Vermont, campus. Later, through our Java U to You program, we brought a curriculum covering coffee and the business of coffee to select customer locations, too. (Similarly, but on a much larger scale, the multinational alcoholic beverage company Diageo runs Diageo Bar Academy, offering in-person and virtual classes to help bartenders and owners of food and drink establishments to level up their knowledge and skills and stay on top of industry trends.[6])

We wanted wholesale customers to understand and appreciate coffee at the level we did, to share in the satisfaction of selling a product that we all felt good about, and to be more successful at selling it. Bringing customers to our "home" in Vermont was an immersion course in our company culture. We offered visitors tours of our operations, of course—and made sure that people visiting connected personally with folks they might have only dealt with on the phone. We talked up our environmental and community engagement programs, with the hope that others might adopt them for their workplaces, too. And we always asked visitors to share their impressions of what they saw—a really useful way of reflecting our culture back to us, showing where we might yet improve.

As we acquired significant wholesale customers, we had some rather large groups coming through little Waterbury. In the late 1990s, we invited the entire management group from Nestlé Waters to attend Coffee College. They distributed our coffee in the important office market. When they arrived at our doorstep in four separate tour buses, it made a big impression! Since Waterbury didn't yet have a big hotel of its own, we had to arrange for guests to stay in nearby

Stowe or Burlington. In fiscal year 2001, we welcomed more than 400 employees of Green Mountain wholesale customers to learn at our on-campus Java University.

Our focus on customer education and engagement established us as an authority, and showed customers who we were and what we cared about. Today, thanks in part to the popularity of subscription business models, especially in enterprise software, customer education is a strategic imperative for many businesses. IBM Cloud, for example, assigns its B2B customers a team of specialists that trains them on the best applications for their business, and regularly seeks feedback to improve its products, which contributes to the company's high customer retention rate.[7] It's not just software companies that are embracing customer education, though. A survey by market-intelligence firm IDC found that in the manufacturing industry, for example, customer education programs helped firms improve an average 24 percent across key measures, including product ROI, customer onboarding, brand awareness, and product or feature adoption.[8]

SaaS companies—including HubSpot, Slack, Salesforce, Workday, and Zendesk—have been leaders in forging in-person connections with their business customers, too, hosting big annual or biannual user conferences that combine workshops, product demos, entertainment, and networking opportunities. Salesforce's annual customer event, Dreamforce, has become a massive annual celebration that embodies founder Marc Benioff's Hawaiian-inspired *ohana* philosophy—the idea that all stakeholders in the company should be thought of as family. The event drew more than 40,000 people to downtown San Francisco in fall 2023.[9] Since 2007, Workday, a maker of cloud-based software for financial management, human resources, and enterprise resource planning, has hosted its Workday Rising event, which now features hundreds of speakers and in 2023 had 15,000 people attending the event in San Francisco, plus many more attending virtually.[10]

It's interesting to note the strong correlation between the investment that these companies make in customer education and their high rankings for employee satisfaction—indeed they seem to be mutually reinforcing. A 2021 joint study by Forbes Insights and Salesforce, for example, found that companies that focus on both customer experience and employee experience saw their revenues grow almost twice as fast as those that focus exclusively on one or the other.[11]

We had many customer events over the years at Green Mountain, but the biggest one was in the mid-1990s, when we invited about 200 customers to Waterbury, some of whom had been with us for well over a decade. Ron Clausen, the manager of the Holiday Inn in Waterbury, a longtime Green Mountain customer, presented arriving guests with a special room key card, stenciled with a Green Mountain logo. We marked off parking spaces in a field, not with painted lines or cones, but with rows of painted coffee beans. At an event held in a big tent behind our buildings, we recognized customers with gorgeous Lucite plaques we had specially made, calling the customers up on stage in the order of the length of time each had been with us.

"That was one of the most emotional days at Green Mountain ever," recalls Rick Peyser, who had started our mail-order business in 1987 and later went on to run our social advocacy and coffee community outreach programs. "The employees were all standing on chairs, clapping and cheering. They were really happy to see long-term customers recognized." It was truly a celebration of what we had accomplished together—and it left an impression on our customers. Just as important, it reminded employees that they were part of a special place, too.

BUILD ON STRENGTHS

As our efforts through the 1990s led to tremendous growth in our retail business, it became ever more apparent that retail was the part of our business that no longer fit. Looking at what really worked well in our company, where we were at our best, we determined it was our burgeoning wholesale business, where our unmatched ability to execute as a team and create value for, and with, our customers set us apart from competitors.

By the mid-1990s, Green Mountain had a dozen cafés—in Vermont, Connecticut, Maine, Massachusetts, New Hampshire, New York, and Illinois. A few of them were successful. But the majority failed to turn a profit. And by this time, the exposure our brand was getting through wholesale channels was far more significant than the impressions we were making through our own retail locations.

It's sexy to have your brand on the street. But retail was extremely hard for us—we were constantly dealing with people issues, and the stores had lots of merchandise to order and stock. And for a variety of reasons, retail wasn't a good fit for the culture of our business. Starbucks was obsessed with the retail customer experience in a way that we never would be. Part of the principle of "sustaining an opportunity mindset" is being aware of the need to make a shift in order to continue bringing a larger vision to life—and having the courage to do it.

In 1998, we made the tough but necessary decision to shut down all our company-owned cafés. "This was a split board decision," recalls longtime board member Bill Davis. "But we decided we didn't have the retail model. It was costing too much money, and it wasn't reproducible. It made more sense to focus our strategies elsewhere." The hardest part was that retail had a lot of employees, relatively speaking—about half of the company's total headcount at the time. Shuttering the stores meant saying goodbye to friends, and of course roiled some people in the organization. We sold many of the stores to their managers, who kept their employees on staff—and in most cases, those stores became more profitable. And we moved many employees who supported retail operations to other positions in the company.

Chasing retail could have mired us for years if we had stubbornly stuck with it. Acknowledging that we were just better at something else was critical to moving forward, allowed us to focus our energies in the areas where we were strongest, and laid the foundation for even bigger opportunities still ahead.

LESSONS TO GO

Tailor the product experience. Invest in understanding the elements of customer success in a given product or service category, and surprise and delight customers with targeted point-of-sale solutions, training, and other support.

Use systems and technology to support information sharing and collaboration. Working well together is a competitive edge in any business, and understanding key metrics helps you focus on what's most important.

Go where competitors won't. Not many coffee companies wanted to go head-to-head with Dunkin' Donuts in the market for "roadside coffee." But by sustaining an opportunity mindset, we recognized the possibilities and transformed them into profitable outcomes.

Sell success. Don't talk about price until customers have tried your product or service—and understand how it will make them more successful. The key question is "How much can we sell?," not "What does it cost?"

Bring customers into the fold. Share information, education, and in-person experiences to support customers, build relationships, and co-create success.

Make success everyone's job. Great teams work together to share work and create solutions. This helps your customers and builds pride and fulfillment among your employees.

Show your commitment to quality in every interaction. The value of your offering comes from the perception of quality created by every touchpoint with your brand. Educate and empower employees at all levels to represent and advocate for the standards of your organization, no matter what.

Show customers "where you live." Hosting trainings and customer-appreciation events on your home turf gives partners an authentic experience of your company's culture, shows that you value them as stakeholders—and inspires employees by letting them see the impact of their work.

Keep it personal. Consider carefully the cost versus benefit of outsourcing customer-facing services. In an increasingly virtual world, in-person interactions provide invaluable opportunities for building customer relationships.

Build on strengths. Keep an eye on what's working, and move toward lines of business where you have unique advantages.

4

PUTTING THE "GREEN" IN GREEN MOUNTAIN

Pursuing a Higher Purpose That Motivates and Energizes Employees and Stakeholders

For most of our first decade at Green Mountain, we were motivated by survival. We worked hard so that we could become profitable and claim our place in an expanding coffee industry. But what really sustained our growth over the long run—and set us apart from competitors—was the motivational power of pursuing a higher purpose, one of the key principles in our Better and Better Blueprint.

Our social and environmental programs earned us accolades, opened new business channels, and enhanced our corporate image and credibility. They differentiated our product for consumers in the marketplace. Most important, they turbocharged employee engagement and enhanced our sense of community—making us a place where people wanted to work, and work hard, because they were contributing to something bigger than just a bottom-line business. I learned that "making the world a better place" was far more motivating than simply making money.

As I write, employers in the United States and around the world are confronting a workforce that wants to make a difference; people—and younger workers, especially—don't want to work just anywhere. In Deloitte's 2023 Gen Z and Millennial Survey, roughly 4 in 10 respondents said they had rejected a job or assignment because it did not align with their values.[1] In the same study, 50 percent of Gen Zs and 46 percent of millennials said they or their colleagues are pressuring businesses to act on climate change.

Our leadership on sustainability, organic and Fair Trade certification, and social programs benefiting partner communities around the world made us pioneers. While it was hardly conventional wisdom at the time, it didn't take long for us to see that purpose and profit went hand in hand. Green Mountain was on *Sustainable Business*'s "World's

Top 20 Sustainable Business Stocks" list annually from 2002 to 2007. In 2006, we were voted the number one best corporate citizen, a Top 10 Best Places to Work, and a top sustainable-business stock.[2] At the time, we were growing revenue at 40 to 50 percent year over year.

The success of our social and environmental programs—our company's higher purpose—stemmed from the fact that they emerged out of authentic employee engagement. We defined and co-created the agenda with Green Mountain employees leading the way. My most important contribution, at first, was creating a work environment where employees had an open invitation to come forward with ideas—things that could make us more profitable or help us do the right thing in our communities.

Like so many things at the company, our social and environmental programs started informally, as an employee-led effort. I didn't create a committee. I didn't tell people what to care about. But by allowing employee enthusiasm to manifest itself in concrete ways, and by throwing company resources behind people's efforts, we created a new sense of urgency and purpose throughout every part of our business.

TAP INTO EMPLOYEE ENTHUSIASM

Sometime in 1989, in one of our regular Friday meetings, Paul Comey—whom I'd first brought in as a roasting equipment consultant and who was now acting as our plant manager—mentioned that a group of employees wanted to form an Environmental Committee. In his role, Paul was often the person to bring me news from the front lines of our operations—what people working in our roasting, packaging, and distribution groups were talking about. Paul explained to me that the employees wanted to look at ways we could be a more environmentally friendly business. Mike Pelchar, our wholesale account service manager, was their informal leader.

I was impressed with the initiative and encouraged them to get started. From the beginning, "doing the right thing"—helping each other, helping in the community, helping customers—was a core

Green Mountain value. I'd always allowed and encouraged employees to pursue volunteer projects of their choosing and gave them time to do so. People worked at the local food bank, built houses with Habitat for Humanity, or helped answering phones during fund-raisers for the public radio station. (I'll discuss our volunteer programs in detail in Chapter 5.) The creation of an internal environmental group seemed like another instance of employees wanting to do good. There was a growing popular awareness that the environment was hurting and that our company should help. Mike—an upbeat and enthusiastic guy—seemed like a good person to lead the group.

In Vermont, a rural state where people enjoy lots of outdoor activities, the environment was something people were already passionate about. So this wasn't an entirely new direction for us. Before the foundation of the Environmental Committee, we had implemented composting and recycling programs. But the formation of the committee, led by employees, made us go from just "caring about the environment" to putting coordinated programs in place.

The committee set its own agenda and decided how to execute it. I didn't need to sign off on most of the early initiatives the committee members were proposing. People knew that as long as they weren't breaking laws or spending outrageous amounts of money, they could go ahead and move on ideas that improved processes and made us more profitable or efficient (or both), and work with their direct managers to implement them. We were running two shifts, and empowering people to make improvements on the fly was just part of our DNA. People who thrived at Green Mountain, generally, were people who liked taking the initiative and pulling in others to help them figure things out.

Within a few years, the Environmental Committee, comprising a dozen or so people from across the company, could already point to numerous important accomplishments. The committee implemented changes that cut our waste stream in half, and in 1994, we joined the national BuyRecycled! Business Alliance, pledging to document and increase our purchases of recycled goods every year. We changed shipping boxes to use less material and started using chemical-free cornstarch-based foam peanuts, which decompose in water, to protect products during shipping. We switched to oxygen-whitened coffee filters instead of standard bleached filters and started selling these dioxin- and chlorine-free earth-friendly coffee filters to the public. We found a bunch of uses for the burlap bags that our green coffee beans came in, giving them away locally for gardening and crafts. When we built a new computer room, we made sure it had a cutting-edge heat-recovery system. (Later, in 1999, we installed a 95-kilowatt cogeneration unit in our roasting facility, which reduced the amount of propane we needed for roasting and also generated electricity. It had the added benefit of reducing the risk of fires created by power outages.)

Apart from these tangible accomplishments, the most significant outcome of the Environmental Committee's work was the incredible level of engagement it created across the company. People were a lot more conscientious about doing things that saved money when they were good for the environment, and that was noticeable right away. In the mid-1980s, I remember trying to get people to turn off the lights and turn down the heat at night, for example. When they understood this as a little thing that they could do to make us a little more profitable, we made very little progress in changing behavior. When the employee-led Environmental Committee put out the same message but presented it as something we could do to help the environment, we had a remarkably different result. People started turning down the heat so much at night that the pipes were in danger of freezing during the winter. We actually had to put locks on some of the thermostats to prevent that. Winter nights in Vermont are no joke!

I was aware that a few other companies were similarly focused— Tom's of Maine is one that stands out in my mind. Tom's of Maine was a pioneer in achieving sustainable product sourcing and packaging, in encouraging employee volunteering, and in contributing a portion of profits to environmental and social causes.[3] It wasn't conventional wisdom at the time that you should implement such programs. Now, we know that this is a better way of doing business, borne out again and again in research on companies pursuing environmental, social, and governance principles. ESG issues were first mentioned in the 2006 United Nations Principles for Responsible Investment report—and 63 investment companies signed on. As of June 2019, there were 2,450 signatories, representing over $80 trillion in assets under management.[4]

A 2022 study of nearly 1,300 global companies by the Centre for Economics and Business Research/Moore Global found that companies embracing ESG principles in recent years enjoyed higher revenues, stronger profit growth, and greater access to finance. The same study found that between 2019 and 2022, ESG companies saw revenue growth of 9.7 percent, versus 4.5 percent for companies that disregarded ESG considerations. In 2022, 96 percent of G250 companies reported on sustainability and ESG matters.[5]

Researchers suggest numerous reasons for the superior performance of ESG-focused organizations. Chief among them are much higher rates of engagement on the part of both consumers and employees. In the 2023 IBM Institute for Business Value survey, about two-thirds of consumers said that both environmental sustainability and social responsibility were very or extremely important to them.[6] Most survey respondents said they would rather work for a company they consider to be socially responsible (71 percent) and environmentally sustainable (69 percent), and nearly half would even do so for less money.

From our first ad hoc initiatives, as the company grew, our sustainability and social betterment programs became more ambitious, far-reaching, and formalized. The company's wholehearted support, from the very beginning, for a mission that employees themselves had chosen helped them see Green Mountain as not just a vibrant workplace, but a place where they could make a difference in the world, where they could feel good about what they did, and where they were motivated to keep getting better and better. We would not have succeeded the way we did without this fundamental shared outlook.

PURSUE THE HIGHEST STANDARDS

The Environmental Committee initially focused on our operations in Vermont and across the United States. But it wasn't long before Green Mountain started to think more broadly about issues of sustainability, as well as social equity, throughout the supply chain. Coffee is the world's biggest beverage commodity, and about 125 million people depend on it for their livelihood. The vast majority of them are small farmers in the developing world. We had a unique opportunity to impact not just the environment, but also local coffee economies all over the world.

In the early 1990s, we started buying excellent coffee beans from William "Bill" McAlpin, who owned a coffee farm called Hacienda La Minita in Tarrazú, Costa Rica. Bill was a pioneer in the concept of "estate coffee," which was grown, harvested, milled, and prepared for export under one roof—a new concept at the time. Bill was a passionate advocate for the value of his land and the people who worked it.

Inspired by Bill, we developed what we called our Stewardship line of coffee—which proclaimed "respect for the land and workers"—purchasing a portion of our coffee from farms and cooperatives in Mexico, Hawaii, Peru, Guatemala, and Sumatra that limited their use of herbicides and pesticides and put soil-erosion controls in place. (In coffee-growing regions around the world, the practice of clear-cutting forests to make way for coffee farms was all too common.) Additionally, these farms provided housing, medical assistance, and other kinds of support to their employees. We paid a higher price for this coffee, rewarding farmers who embraced these more earth-friendly—and compassionate—practices.

We asked Bill to come to several of our stores to talk with staff and do promotions for store customers. From these experiences, we learned that consumers both understood the importance of coffee-sourcing practices and also felt that our efforts to produce coffee in ways that were more beneficial to our partners made it more "special." It added to their general appreciation of our product and its quality.

Educating customers about what we were doing was therefore key to differentiating ourselves as a company.

When we first began the Stewardship program, we were basically writing our own rules—there were no industry, national, or international guidelines or standards. But as we started to think more broadly about sustainability and social equity throughout our supply chain, we sought out third-party organizations with the expertise to ensure that the work we did and the labels we placed on our products were meaningful. We worked with Conservation International to develop our Stewardship standards. And with the nonprofit Rainforest Alliance, we introduced Rainforest Nut Coffee—a hazelnut-flavored coffee—to promote awareness of and raise money to fight tropical deforestation.

It wasn't long before others in the industry started developing their own programs. It became a confusing landscape for consumers, with no real way to compare what different companies were doing. We realized that it would be important to get a third party with an established trusted standard to verify that our coffee hit the mark. We sold some organic coffee as early as 1989. But as certification standards became more formalized, we doubled down on getting our farmer partners and our facilities certified to the latest standards; and in 1997, we introduced our first organic, farm-direct coffee from Peru, produced in our own fully organic-certified production facility.

Patty Vincent—an energetic, brown-haired, brown-eyed animal lover with a degree in anthropology, who started out as a server in the original Green Mountain Coffee store—was our coffee product manager. She took charge of helping us secure our official organic certification. "We had to have integrity to sell these coffees with all these seals," she recollects. "If we were asking farmers to sell us organic coffee, we had to follow through and get certified as organic, also. I was able to go all over the country meeting with different organic groups, and I learned a great deal."

Organic certification essentially deals with how food and other commodities, such as cotton, are grown and produced. It doesn't address issues like labor, free association, and human rights. Fair Trade certification does. A rigorous, globally recognized program, Fair Trade ensured that producers of commodities including coffee and cocoa had safe working conditions, earned a fair income, and were able to build stronger communities, all while protecting the environment. Regular monitoring helped ensure compliance and transparency. Coffee was an important focus of the movement because it is such a widely traded commodity and comes almost universally from economically developing countries. If you work in the coffee industry and you're selling coffee for four bucks, knowing that most farmers do not make enough money to live on doesn't feel very good.

Fair Trade certification seemed a logical next step in our work to support our coffee suppliers, helping us pursue a higher purpose and value all stakeholders, key principles in the Better and Better Blueprint. The Fair Trade certification put an official stamp of approval on much of what we were already doing, both in our Stewardship program and in our work with other programs like the nonprofit Coffee Kids, which sponsored a microlending program in the area around Huatusco, Mexico, to support small family businesses and diversify local economies dependent on coffee growing. Several employees recall with amusement how surprised they were by my enthusiasm in a 1999 meeting at Green Mountain's headquarters with Fair Trade's Kimberly Easton, when—even before she could complete her sales pitch—I'd put my fist down on the table and declared, "We're doing it!" People said they had never seen me so excited.

In 2000, Green Mountain became one of the first major US coffee companies to sign up with Fair Trade USA, committing to purchase coffee at a minimum "floor" price from small farmer cooperatives in Peru, Mexico, Guatemala, and Sumatra. Paul Rice, who founded Fair Trade USA in 1998 and still leads the organization, remembers: "Green Mountain was, up until that point, the largest company that we were wooing. The other companies that had come on board in those first two years were much smaller roasters. When Green Mountain signed with Fair Trade, our organization was only two years old, and nobody had proven that you could make the [business model] work."

Our pursuit of Fair Trade certification also reflected our deep belief in sustaining an opportunity mindset—one of the seven pillars of the Better and Better Blueprint. Doing Fair Trade was going to take a lot of work and require additional financial investments. It would impact the economics of our business. But it was the right thing to do, *and* we were confident it would only drive further business success by positively setting us apart in the industry. Our commitment to Fair Trade, and to all our initiatives aimed at "doing good," was motivated by caring and compassion, but also our desire, as ambitious entrepreneurs, to achieve additional competitive advantage.

Knowing we wanted to make at least 3 percent of all our sales Fair Trade certified, we started with the line of 10 organic whole-bean coffees we already sold, making sure those met all Fair Trade standards. In some cases, that just meant we had to pay our existing suppliers more money. In other cases, though, it meant we had to switch suppliers altogether. But adding the Fair Trade label really made a difference: In our first year with the Fair Trade label, sales on the organic line jumped 15 percent. As we added more Fair Trade offerings, it sent a powerful signal to the rest of the market, and major competitors started following our lead. But none came close to the percentage of Fair Trade business that Green Mountain did.

Implementing Fair Trade was not without its challenges, especially for those in the company who had to operationalize and sell it. One challenge that our cross-functional "coffee team" had to deal with was the decision to sell our Fair Trade coffee at the same price as our other "regular" beans. My goal was not just to offer Fair Trade coffee as a sideshow, but to help build a broader market for it. Since we sold the greatest volume of coffee through supermarket partners, getting their buy-in was essential. A number of our supermarket accounts liked to sell coffee in self-serve plastic bins, where all the coffees were priced the same. Fair Trade, of course, cost us more, but to build sales volume and keep things simple for the supermarkets, we took a smaller margin on it. But with the right combination of lower-cost beans and higher-cost ones, we were able to average it out.

The benefits of Fair Trade far outweighed the drawbacks. Our commitment to certified organic and Fair Trade coffee not only differentiated us from competitors and stoked tremendous pride within the company; it also created partnership opportunities we never could have imagined. In October 2002, for example, we signed a 10-year agreement to be the exclusive roaster, seller, and distributor for Newman's Own organic and Fair Trade–certified coffees, which helped us to acquire new supermarket accounts and, finally, attain nationwide distribution of our bagged coffee.[7] Thanks in large part to this relationship, by 2003, we were one of the largest sellers of "double-certified"—organic and Fair Trade—coffee in the world. In 2005, the Newman's Own partnership got us into more than 600 McDonald's locations in New England and upstate New York as their "house" coffee, another huge boost for regional brand recognition.

Success brought criticism, as well. I heard from people both within and outside the company that we didn't go far enough. If we believed in Fair Trade, then why sell any coffee that didn't meet these standards? I argued that the more successful we could be as a business, the more we could realize our mission to do good. If we were selling only Fair Trade coffee—a premium product—we couldn't have gotten a customer like the food services giant Sodexo, which started distributing Green Mountain coffee in the Northeast United States in 2002. Even better: Just two years after we started doing business with Sodexo, it did start buying Fair Trade coffee from us—and lots of it—helping us gain a much bigger footprint in the college market. If we hadn't started doing business with the folks at Sodexo, we never could have developed a working relationship and helped them understand Fair Trade's benefits.

In time, Fair Trade came to represent nearly 30 percent of Green Mountain's total coffee purchases and sales, leading to more high-profile collaborations that burnished our reputation as a socially responsible business—and reinforced for employees that they worked at a special place. A great example of this is our partnership with Jane Goodall, the naturalist, to launch a coffee with beans grown in the area surrounding her chimpanzee preserve in Tanzania. The idea was to provide a legal source of income for locals—an alternative to the hunting of monkeys and chimps for bushmeat and exotic pets.

In the course of working out the deal, Rick Peyser, who was our director of coffee community outreach, Laura Peterson in marketing, and our coffee manager Lindsey Bolger and her seven-year-old son went to visit some of the farms in person. Afterward, they had the unforgettable experience of crossing Lake Tanganyika to visit Goodall's home. Lindsey remembers: "We arrived by boat at the Gombe Stream National Park as the sun was setting over the lake, and there's Jane Goodall sitting with her colleagues in camp chairs on the beach, around a campfire sipping Famous Grouse. And we were invited to join the party. It was one of many 'pinch me' moments in my career at Green Mountain." It was a truly moving experience when Goodall visited our Waterbury headquarters on September 19, 2007, for a special event marking the launch of the coffee we'd developed together with the Jane Goodall Institute.

Participating in the Fair Trade movement could be as simple as buying from an approved supplier and paying the premium. But we went much deeper. We did joint trainings around quality control, and flew coffee-farm leaders from around the world to Vermont to sit around a table with Green Mountain people to slurp and spit the coffee and calibrate their taste buds. This increased their capacity not only to meet our specifications but to meet gourmet or specialty specifications in general.

In 2002, we became the first corporate investor in a nonprofit microloan organization called Root Capital, providing millions of dollars in loans to cash-strapped coffee farmers. In the same year, we formed an alliance with the US Agency for International Development to improve the livelihoods of those in impoverished coffee-growing regions. In 2003, *Business Ethics* magazine ranked us number 8 on its list of the 100 Best Corporate Citizens, putting us alongside the likes of General Mills, Intel, IBM, and Starbucks (below us, at number 21). In 2006—the year after we released our first corporate social responsibility report—we were number 1.[8] We repeated that feat the next year. (In the 2000s, we hosted several of these companies at a mini-summit on sustainability at our Vermont campus—an amazing honor given how relatively tiny we were.) These recognitions were huge for morale and engagement within our company.

But from the very beginning, our leadership in implementing CSR programs gave us an outsized influence in the corporate world, beyond the coffee industry. In the early 1990s, for example, we were invited to become part of an unofficial group of 25 companies, called Eco Partners, that wanted to lead on environmental issues. Each company sent one or two people to semiannual weekend-long meetings to share best practices and talk about experiences with various nonprofit partners. This was a remarkable opportunity for co-creating excellence alongside esteemed business peers. The member companies would take turns hosting, on the East Coast in the fall and the West Coast in the spring. The expertise we had acquired through our leadership in the coffee world—which really started with the Environmental Committee—put us at the same table as senior-level people from companies including Patagonia, Starbucks, L.L. Bean, Timberland, and Ben & Jerry's. "The camaraderie and the contacts we got from that were invaluable," Paul Comey remembers.

It all stemmed from our pursuit of a higher purpose and our commitment to valuing all our stakeholders—and the energy and knowledge that flowed back into our company rekindled our commitment to doing better still.

CELEBRATE YOUR MISSION TO ATTRACT LIKE MINDS

Marketing sustainability and social mission is tricky. Research has shown that people will buy products from a company that's doing good, but I never wanted it to appear that we were doing these things just to make a sale. Similar to the way that supporting customer success was key to our wholesale coffee business, I believed the best way to promote our own brand and values was by promoting the nonprofit organizations and others we partnered with.

When our Rainforest Nut Coffee came out, for example, we used the packaging to promote the benefits of rainforest preservation for fighting climate change. By explaining why we were doing this, the aim was to get others to take up the cause, too. To promote the Fair Trade movement, among other things, we designed a coffee truck—the Green Mountain Mobile—that would go around to concerts and festivals, giving away free organic Fair Trade coffee. If you were at a big event in Vermont in the early 2000s, you saw us.

We were also the lead sponsor of a concert series with major musical artists, partnering with singers Kelly Clarkson and Michael Franti to promote the benefits of Fair Trade. This collaborative effort demonstrates the Better and Better Blueprint concept of sharing positive experiences of our brand to win hearts and engage minds. These concerts weren't about paying artists who didn't care one way or another about the issues to promote our brand. We made sure they cared—sending Kelly on a trip to see Fair Trade cooperatives in Colombia with Paul Rice from Fair Trade USA and sending Michael to visit farms in Sumatra.[9] After these experiences, it doesn't surprise me that both these artists became passionate Fair Trade advocates.

Our association with these artists helped us connect with important audiences of young, impressionable customers. For a year, at every concert, Michael would talk about Fair Trade and mention Green Mountain. That was also a huge rush for employees who went to these shows. There was a great sense of "Hey, we did this!" and of being part of something vital and meaningful. You really can't overestimate the value of working for a company that you're proud of—and helping to make a product that your favorite performers are celebrating onstage.

Paul has spoken with me about the impact this had for Fair Trade: "Our consumer awareness numbers jumped dramatically during those years that Green Mountain was doing those national campaigns with artists like Kelly and Michael." As awareness of our work on sustainability and stewardship spread, it also helped us attract talent from competitors—people who were more passionate than your average job seeker. A standout in that regard was Lindsey Bolger, who became our coffee manager—in charge of coffee quality, development, and procurement—in 2001.

Lindsey, who had long, straight light-brown hair and a smile that put people at ease, came from a small but highly regarded coffee roaster called Batdorf & Bronson in Olympia, Washington. She was really cause-driven, passionate about helping coffee-growing communities better their living conditions, improve education for their kids, and embrace more sustainable farming practices. She was a little leery about joining a big company, but she also knew our reputation and the work we were doing. And we were able to convince her that by coming to Green Mountain, she could leverage her position to support these causes more than ever. "I was very happy with my life in Washington State and really had no intentions of leaving my situation," Lindsey remembers. "But Green Mountain was always my benchmark—they had a similar foundational principle, a similar ethos, but on a much larger scale. And I had come to know and really respect folks in the company and how they brought so much of themselves, so much of their passion, so much of their grounded approach to maneuvering in the world of business to the company."

Without our larger mission, we probably never would have attracted someone as talented as Lindsey, or the many other people who came seeking a place where they could work without leaving their values at the door. Lindsey took the job and found it even more fulfilling than she expected. "I was responsible for coffee quality, supply chain development, procurement—everything up stream of roasting—in addition to product development," she recounted at a recent gathering of former Green Mountain folks. "But the work became about so much more than that. To unravel this very twisted path from farm to cup, to look under the hood and understand how it works and learn the stories of all those involved, that was all part of the appeal."

Lindsey also "did well by doing good" through our stock purchase program, and was able to buy a new place for her mother when shares soared from 2008 to 2011. After her retirement from Green Mountain in 2017, she continued to do good work by serving on the board of Root Capital and Food 4 Farmers and as an advisor to Fair

Trade USA, as well as driving for Meals on Wheels, serving seniors in her community. A Green Mountain employee through and through!

SHARE EXPERIENCES TO GET BUY-IN

The best way to really understand something, I've long insisted, is to experience it for yourself. Consistently and creatively sharing positive experiences of our brand was integral to our success, and I would come to see it as a core principle in the Better and Better Blueprint. That's why I was so obsessed with giving consumers opportunities to taste our coffee. And it's why, starting in 1991, we sent hundreds of Green Mountain employees on company-sponsored trips to visit the farms that we got our coffee from, spending millions of dollars to do so. For many people who worked with us over the years, these trips stand out as a highlight of their time at the company. Nobody who went was left untouched by the experience. For some, it was truly life changing. A key element in our company's success was engaging employees and suppliers to create a caring community, where people on both sides went out of their way to help each other. These "trips to source," which took employees to Central America, Africa, and Asia, were a primary means of achieving that.

These were definitely not luxury vacations. They were sometimes-grueling journeys that typically involved hands-on volunteer work, as well as hours spent picking coffee in the field. Civil unrest and a degree of lawlessness were not unusual in the places we visited. In Guatemala, for example, a lot of the local plantations had militias of ex-soldier types who would patrol the perimeters and schools. But these were the conditions our suppliers lived and worked in, and I believed strongly that you really had to experience something to understand it.

This wasn't "time off"—employees would get their regular pay, and we would cover travel expenses, lodging, transport, and everything else. We set up a nomination committee to choose who would go—it was sort of a reward for doing well in your job. And we would try to bring people from different parts of the company in on the same trip to allow people to establish relationships with others in the organization, understanding not only their jobs but who they were as people. I was really insistent that the opportunity should be open to everyone—whether it was a receptionist, someone in sales, or someone who worked in our packaging plant. As we got bigger and bigger, anything we could do to keep building that sense of community was so valuable.

The first trip took a group to our friend Bill McAlpin's La Minita estate in Costa Rica. Later, we'd go to other countries in Central and South America, Africa, and Southeast Asia. The groups could range from a dozen or so people to about 25. At first, we'd do this once a year. As we started growing quicker, in order to share this experience with more people, we did three or four trips a year. At one point, we figured out that more than 20 percent of the company had gone.

Although I'm not an avid world traveler, I went, too—not on the first trip, but on the second one, and several times after that, to Guatemala, Costa Rica, and Mexico. On one trip I went on, we took Nell Newman, the daughter of actors Paul Newman and Joanne Woodward, who started the Newman's Own Organics division of the Newman's Own brand. Even before we sold coffee to Newman's, we'd developed a coffee blend to help support the Hole in the Wall Gang Camp, a nonprofit founded by her dad in 1988 to provide opportunities for kids with serious illnesses to have a real summer-camp experience.

Seeing the needs of our source farmers firsthand, and their eagerness to do well and make good, was incredibly moving. What do you say to somebody who says, "I just want to provide for my family. What should I do? Can I learn something? Is there something I can work on?" As much as I knew about poverty and living conditions in these countries, learning about the lack of things like clean water through lived experience makes it so much more personal. It compels you to do more.

Some of our employees who went on our trips to source countries had never been on a plane before. Some had never even been outside of Vermont. It could be overwhelming. Lynne Herbert, who joined the company in 2005 and transformed our IT department, went on one of the trips to Nicaragua. "I didn't know what to expect," she remembers. "We were in places with dirt floors, where they cooked over fire, and in order to serve meals for us, some family members would go without eating. The families were proud and would have been insulted if we'd offered to pay them for extra food."

On that trip, Lynne recalls, "The farmers were incredible—they didn't want us to feel sorry for them. We harvested coffee beans with them, wearing these baskets around our waists, marching up the mountain, having a competition to see who could pick the most." Their welcoming attitude reminded my assistant, Diane, of people back home: "Vermont people tend to be open and friendly. It was the same thing there. It made you feel like you had a responsibility to treat the coffee well at our end." Our employees were amazed to see the way that we were welcomed—like rock stars—because of the work people like Rick and others had been doing in these countries already. When they arrived in a new town, the Green Mountain van would be swarmed by farmers and their families, wearing hats and T-shirts with our logo that we'd given them on past visits. (Rick's 2016 book, *Brewing Change*, chronicles his career with Green Mountain working on Fair Trade and other programs supporting coffee farmers.)

I saw the energy from our trips flow back into the company. It showed up in a heightened respect for the product and the people who supplied it, changing the way we thought about every interaction with our coffee. Diane recalls: "The roasters, Curtis and that group, took it personally that they get the roasting profile just right and produce high-quality coffee. They felt a responsibility to the people who farmed the coffee. That idea permeated the company." Rick Peyser recalls: "After our first trip, I felt so bad spilling even a few beans as I was scooping. I knew how much work was involved to get those few beans." Similar to the way people became obsessed with turning down the heat when they understood it as helpful for the environment, after these trips, employees who worked with coffee became obsessive about waste, knowing how much work was involved in getting it here.

Versions of our trips to source exist in other companies and industries, too, as a way to reward employees and build stronger supply chain connections. Employees at Whole Foods Market, for example, can apply to travel to communities around the world where the company sources products or funds microcredit clients through its Whole Planet Foundation.[10] In an example closer to home for me, Hotel Vermont, a boutique hotel in Burlington with a noted food and beverage program—sends employees to visit the producers supplying its restaurant. "Knowing your farmer"—and having them know you—has benefits for businesses of any size. As more and more work interactions become virtual, the impact of face-to-face time and shared experience is more powerful than ever.

BRING THE EXPERIENCE BACK HOME

When you send people to experience things outside your organization, make sure to bring that learning back inside and promote the outcomes you are achieving. When employees came back from trips to origin countries, they would always share their experiences—in stories and pictures—at our companywide meetings. Hearing directly from peers, and sensing their genuine enthusiasm and emotion, really brought home the idea that there was a bigger purpose to what we were all doing.

We'd have coffee farmers come to Vermont, too, showing them our production process and including them in "cupping" sessions to share how we evaluated the final product, and we'd have them speak to employees about the impact of our work on their lives. These presentations could get very emotional, and the experience built trust and increased commitment on both sides.

On one trip to Mexico, a crew from the news show *Frontline* came along to do a feature on Fair Trade. On the first day, one of the producers was walking around this little town in Mexico and said something like, "I don't see a story here." But after a few days visiting with coffee farmers, members of the crew said it was the most life-changing story they ever worked on. What was going to be a 4-minute story ended up being a 20-minute segment. But the real significance of the story is that the reporter working on this news assignment actually came from Mexico City, and he had no idea of the working and living conditions that people so nearby were experiencing. He had to see for himself.

We'd also bring board members, and sometimes potential customers, on "origin trips," with equally powerful results. In the early 2000s, for example, we brought Perry Odak, then head of Wild Oats—later acquired by Whole Foods—on a several-day trip to visit coffee farmers in the Veracruz region of Mexico. At the time, Wild Oats was the second-largest natural foods market in the country, after Whole Foods; and Odak had a reputation as a hard-boiled business guy, a turnaround guy. He'd been CEO of Ben & Jerry's when it was acquired by Unilever. We were hoping to get him interested in selling our coffee.

Paul Rice from Fair Trade USA, who also came on this trip, has a vivid recollection of the moment when Odak "got it." We were speaking with a farmer named Ysidro in his farmyard—he had three acres of coffee and one acre of corn and beans, a common arrangement for "small-holder" farmers. Paul recounts: "Ysidro had six children. He had only studied through third grade—at age nine his parents pulled him out of school and put him to work in the fields because they needed the extra labor." In the most poignant and humble terms, Ysidro told us about his childhood and his struggles as a fourth-generation coffee farmer, and explained how his family had more money since his coffee cooperative got Fair Trade certified and we started buying from them. Now, he said, three of his kids were in college, and two were in high school—thanks to a scholarship fund that the co-op had set up with the Fair Trade premium. The sixth kid hated school and only wanted to be with his dad working on the farm.

"He was now quite a happy dad," Paul recalls. "He didn't see Fair Trade as charity, but rather as a fair return for all of his hard work to produce the highest-quality coffee he could. As he was talking, I remember looking over at Odak and seeing that he was teary-eyed. It turns out that he'd grown up on a dairy farm in upstate New York and milked cows for his dad as a kid. Under his crusty shell, he had a deep abiding love for farming folk, especially poor farming folk. He could relate to them. It just made me realize that underneath every corporate executive is a human, a whole human with a diversity of life experiences that make them potentially open to seeing the humanity of the workers in their supply chain."

That night at dinner, Odak told me that he wanted all Wild Oats's private-label coffee to be roasted by Green Mountain and to be 100 percent Fair Trade and organic. I honestly hadn't planned this trip to attain this result. I just wanted to show him where the coffee was coming from—and where we were coming from. The genuine shared human experience that this important decision-maker had is what led to this outcome, which, for our business, turned out to be quite significant. Perry Odak was so inspired, he hired artists to create a mural-sized artwork that explained Fair Trade, which he put in every single store. Wild Oats also worked with us on an initiative to construct organic vegetable gardens for coffee growers in rural Mexico. And when Wild Oats was acquired by Whole Foods Markets, that company also became a customer for Fair Trade coffee.[11] And we have Ysidro to thank for that.

DON'T WAIT TO GIVE BACK

In addition to everything we were doing in terms of sustainability, organic certification, and Fair Trade, in fiscal year 1991, the company committed to donating 5 percent of its pretax income—in the form of monetary contributions and product donations—to a range of nonprofit organizations, split roughly 50-50 between communities in the United States and those in coffee-producing countries. And as long as I was in charge of the company, we never wavered from that commitment. Among the organizations that benefited from donations were Conservation International, Rainforest Alliance, the American Red Cross, the United Way, and smaller NGOs like Coffee Kids, as well as schools, counseling centers, soup kitchens, libraries, and religious organizations in markets where Green Mountain operated.

Why 5 percent? Certainly, there are different models out there. Hundreds of businesses have taken the One Percent for the Planet pledge, committing 1 percent of their sales to efforts that preserve and restore the natural environment. When I was coming up with our number, I recall that Tom's of Maine was giving 10 percent.[12] That was probably tied to the Christian concept of tithing, and it seemed a little steep. So 5 percent was halfway to that. In the United States, people give about 2 percent of their income to charity.[13] I wanted to be above average. Five percent seemed reasonable, and enough to have an impact. Your number might be different. The big idea is to pick something that's based in reality and to stick with it.

I chose a percentage of profit before taxes, versus a percentage of sales, for a couple of reasons. We had to be profitable first, and pegging our donations to profit, I felt, would better reflect any efficiencies we gained by doing things more effectively. It also meant that if we had a really terrible, unprofitable year, we'd keep that money for our operations. If we had kept a promise to continue giving while we were losing money, we wouldn't have been able to give for very long.

But a funny thing happened—we became more profitable, not less. We became one of the most profitable independent coffee companies in the United States, in fact. In 2012, we would donate $18.8 million, the largest annual donation we ever made.[14] (It was also the year that company leadership dropped the 5 percent commitment.[15]) While we never quite attained my dream of getting to a hundred million and beating out Coca-Cola—one of the biggest brands in the world—as a percentage of revenue, we had one of the largest corporate giving programs out there.

I regularly had to defend our 5 percent commitment. Bill Davis, a Green Mountain board member and former head of Cabot Cooperative Creamery, recollects: "There was a lot of pressure early on from shareholders and from the board to dramatically decrease that commitment. Today, B corporations, for example, are rewarded for maintaining their commitments. But 15 years ago, we weren't getting positive shareholder feedback as much."

You see these arguments coming up again now, in the form of an "anti-ESG" movement, with critics of social investing attacking financial firms that, say, choose not to invest in the fossil fuel or gun industries. These critics argue that by doing so, these firms are depriving investors—a significant percentage of which are state pension funds—of better returns in pursuit of "woke" values. All that companies should be doing, they argue, is maximizing returns for shareholders. But from the research that's out there, it seems clear that doing well and doing good are far from incompatible: Between 2000 and 2020, stakeholder-focused companies, as a group, saw their shares rise 100 percent higher than the S&P 500.[16]

One of the best examples of a company sticking to its guns in this regard is multibillion-dollar enterprise software pioneer Salesforce, which has established corporate philanthropy as a core part of its DNA through its 1-1-1 model. As an organization, Salesforce donates 1 percent of its product, 1 percent of its equity, and 1 percent of its employees' time to give back to communities worldwide. Since its founding in 1999, the company has reached over half a billion dollars in all-time philanthropic giving.[17]

Seeing a connection between your day-to-day work and the organization's greater impact creates a feeling of values alignment, especially among younger workers. In a survey of workers across the United States by Fidelity Investments, 75 percent of respondents said giving back to the community was the most important benefit of their company's workplace giving program.[18] Today, more companies are embracing models of employee-led giving that are similar to our 5 percent plan. The number two US insurer, Progressive, recently introduced a giving program called Name Your Cause that allows each employee to recommend organizations to receive a $100 donation from the company, even without having to donate themselves.[19] Netflix donates 200 percent of employee donations to organizations of their choosing.[20] Microsoft matches each employee's donations of money, products, and time to nonprofits, up to $15,000 a year.[21]

Our 5 percent commitment to giving at Green Mountain was effectively a way of introducing employees to the concept of giving—and the satisfaction that comes with it—without taking money out of their pockets. As such, it was a key contributor to the culture at Green Mountain—something that made people feel good about where they worked, and by extension, feel good about themselves.

The concept of mirror flourishing, as defined by Case Western Reserve University business school professors David Cooperrider and Ronald Fry, refers to the "consonant flourishing or growing together that happens naturally and reciprocally to us when we actively engage in or witness the acts that help nature flourish, others flourish, or the world as a whole to flourish."[22] In other words, when individuals focus their energy on doing good for others—or just see other people doing good—they activate mechanisms that support their own individual well-being and flourishing.

Like the work of our Environmental Committee, the 5 percent commitment quickly became something that was absolutely integral to our culture. Lindsey Bolger remembers: "Employees were so galvanized by this. We celebrated what we were doing with the 5 percent at every company meeting. People were working hard during this growth period—sprinting like crazy. And you'd think, why am I working on the weekends? Why am I answering email at 11 at night? It's because there was this higher purpose." None of the people in our company wanted that 5 percent for themselves. They wanted it for the farmers' children.

A big point I want to convey to other leaders is that there was never a "good time" to start the 5 percent. There are always sound business reasons not to do it. But I believe that when you do good, good things come your way. People think that karma is some magical, spiritual energy. But really, it just means this: You are where you are because of the decisions you've made. Giving isn't something that you do once you become successful—it's something that you do to become successful.

Striving for a higher good—to be the most sustainable large coffee maker, to make a real difference in the lives of our coffee-growing stakeholders—was central to forging the collaborative, highly engaged culture that we built at Green Mountain. It was something, like the mindfulness training that we offered (more on that in Chapter 5), that allowed people to transcend the day-to-day business of the company and appreciate our larger impact. It made us strive to be better and better, as people, as a community, and as a company.

LESSONS TO GO

Support initiatives that employees care about. An environmental or social mission that's imposed from the top will never engage employees as successfully as one that comes "from within."

Pursue higher standards. It can be more difficult, and usually more expensive, to pursue third-party certifications for sustainable products and ethical business practices—but it can be a big differentiator both for customers and for employees.

Promote your mission, not yourself. Show you care about something by raising awareness of the problems you see and funding promising solutions. That's how you maximize your impact and attract like-minded partners and employees.

Go to the source. Do your employees know where your raw materials come from? Do they know what service providers you rely on? Whatever industry you're in, you can look for opportunities to forge connections and promote empathy across stakeholder groups in your supply chain and to incorporate that new knowledge "back home." Involve board members, other suppliers, and customers, so that they become partners in your success.

Amplify employee giving. Maximize impact and engagement by matching programs and other ways of connecting corporate philanthropy to causes that resonate with employees.

Make realistic, but consistent, commitments. Corporate philanthropy is easy when things are going well. Set a level for giving that you can sustain even in challenging times—and stick with it.

5

OM SHANTI

Promoting Learning, Mindfulness, and Transformative Change

t a celebration of the company's twentieth anniversary in 2001, longtime employee Paul Comey, who had played many roles in the company, leading up to VP of sustainability, presented me with a souvenir that he and other employees had created for the occasion. They'd taken a 10-foot-long, two-person crosscut saw—the old-fashioned kind that loggers used in the 1800s—and mounted it on a board. Along the teeth of the saw, they'd marked off a timeline of big events since Green Mountain was founded: our first donations of coffee to Ronald McDonald House, our first company trip to an origin country, our initial public offering, our investment in Keurig, and so on.

I got a big laugh out of the gift because it was a sly reference to a favorite phrase of mine: "sharpening the saw." That was a metaphor I'd picked up from reading Stephen R. Covey, the self-help guru and author of *The 7 Habits of Highly Effective People*.[1] But for the many Green Mountain employees who'd worked with me over the years, it had become a mantra—a reminder to develop and be mindful of our skills. Covey asks readers to imagine encountering someone working feverishly to cut down a tree in the woods. When you ask what they are doing, they reply impatiently, "I'm sawing down this tree." The woodcutter looks exhausted, so you ask how long they've been working at it. "Over five hours," they reply, "And I'm beat! This is hard work." You suggest they take a few-minute break to sharpen their saw—"I'm sure it would go a lot faster." But the woodcutter replies emphatically: "I don't have time to sharpen the saw. I'm too busy sawing!"

People might laugh and think it's silly that a logger wouldn't know to stop and sharpen the saw. But you see it all the time, in all sorts of other professions, too—people working so hard that they never take time to learn and reflect, to take a course, to read a book for new insights. Maybe they will next week when they aren't so busy, but next week never comes.

On my desk at Green Mountain, I always had piles of books—books on business, sports psychology and performance, meditation, positive affirmations; Deepak Chopra's *The Seven Spiritual Laws of Success*; Louise Hay's *You Can Heal Your Life*—and I enthusiastically gave them out if someone expressed interest. My personal library was a good start when we were a young, small company. But as we grew and faced new challenges in our business, maintaining our competitive edge meant constantly upskilling, learning to better manage work, life, and ourselves.

Almost from the beginning, we offered workshops and trainings in job skills and personal effectiveness practices, which over time grew into a formal Continuous Learning program to which we allocated 3 percent of our budget. We were in all senses a "growth company," where personal and professional growth were intertwined and continuous learning was a core principle. I believed that employees who were well informed about how the business worked would be better partners in helping me run it, and so I never thought of employee training as an expense, but as an investment. And I had the then radical idea that people who felt good about themselves—who had complete, fulfilling lives—would be happier, more engaged employees. These two ideas gave rise to what my former executive assistant called Green Mountain's "aggressive learning environment." Our Continuous Learning programs offered job training and personal-growth opportunities that were unrivaled among companies of any size.

Internal surveys told us that employees valued these learning opportunities, and I believe they helped us work more dynamically—and more happily—together. Coupled with the progressive benefits and incentive programs that we implemented, they helped us to earn a string of workplace awards, including being named to *Forbes* Best Small Companies list seven times.[2]

There's now plenty of research to back up our anecdotal findings from Green Mountain. More than ever, workers today want jobs where they can learn and grow. In the 2023 Work in America Survey conducted by the American Psychological Association (APA), 91 percent of workers said it was very or somewhat important to them to have a job where they consistently had opportunities to learn.[3] The question for leaders is no longer whether to offer continuous learning, but how they can best position their organization as a home for continuous learning, personal growth, well-being, and mindfulness.

CREATE A CONTAGIOUS LEARNING ENVIRONMENT

You can't force employee engagement. Instead, you must create experiences so compelling that employees can't resist wanting to participate. Being a "vibrant workplace"—one that fosters teamwork, fun, personal and professional growth, financial rewards, and work-life balance—was one of our principles, and we wanted our in-house education program to reflect that.

In 2004, we hired Prudence "Pru" Sullivan as our director of continuous learning and organization development, to develop and launch a comprehensive company learning curriculum that would align with the principles that we had co-created through the Appreciative Inquiry process, which I explain in the next chapter. Pru had worked for the Digital Equipment Corporation (DEC), a company in Maynard, Massachusetts, that was an early player in personal computers. DEC had a plant in Vermont, and when the company shut down, she worked for 10 years as an organizational consultant. When the role at our company opened up, Pru was excited to join us and to lead internal transformation. She brought tremendous energy and enthusiasm into launching and growing what was essentially an in-house college.

We put a lot of energy and marketing muscle into pitching our Continuous Learning program to employees. Our first Continuous Learning program catalog, for "academic year" 2005–2006, was a 24-page publication with colorful graphic cover art depicting a coffee bean, planted in the earth, transforming into a seedling—it wasn't unlike the course catalog you might find at a well-funded community college. The offerings included training in sales and marketing, leadership and communication, project management, manufacturing excellence, workplace safety, and various popular software programs. Employees could study Spanish, practice yoga, or learn to meditate.

Except for things like mandatory safety trainings for workers in our plant, we didn't tell employees what they had to learn, but rather aimed to offer multiple learning pathways and demonstrate that we were serious about wanting people to take advantage of them. We asked employees to set development goals—suggesting 20 hours of learning per year—and to look for courses that supported those goals. We made progress toward these goals part of the employees' annual evaluations, and leaders had to build employee learning time into their scheduling.

Starting in 2005, we would hold an annual Continuous Learning Expo at each of our coffee sites, in a festively decorated cafeteria or other large gathering space. Each of our internal programs would set up a table, along with reps for local colleges and national online programs such as University of Phoenix. In later years, Green Mountain staff who had "graduated" from these classes would also help to promote them at the expos. We would distribute each year's new Continuous Learning catalog at the event—but the biggest draw was always food, with wood-fired pizzas being the favorite. There were raffles, and occasionally guest speakers. The theme of our first expo, in 2005, was "When Pigs Fly." "This was a bit tongue in cheek," Pru recalls. "Many organizations talk a good game about investing in employees. We actually meant it. And the battery-operated pigs with wings that hung from the ceiling all over the cafeteria, flying in circles, gave wings to continuous learning as a core principle of the organization."

Today, organizations large and small are strategically prioritizing learning and skills development. Microsoft CEO Satya Nadella, for example, has worked to transform the company into what he calls a "learn-it-all" culture, believing that people—and businesses—with a growth mindset will always perform better.[4] Observing that learning and skills development are often the first things that get pushed aside when people are busy, Nadella has instituted quarterly "learning days," so employees don't need to ask for the time to go and learn something new.

In addition to creating engaging learning opportunities, organizations also need to make learning accessible and inclusive. If you are really prioritizing learning today, you can't stop at in-person, real-time training, but must deploy a range of recorded digital content, virtual classrooms, and other flexible options that allow people to learn on their own schedule and in ways that suit them. In 2007, we started offering a large library of courses on audio CDs—today, you could just download these to your phone!—on everything from professional development to parenting, nutrition, and quitting smoking. The idea was that people could learn during their commute, while relaxing at home, or whenever they were ready and receptive.

There are, of course, numerous socioeconomic barriers to learning that any company with a diverse workforce needs to address as a matter of culture. As we employed more workers outside Vermont, and more nonnative English speakers, we began offering English-as-a-second-language courses for employees and their family members. Green Mountain also provided tuition assistance for people who wanted to pursue outside education opportunities through a community college or an online program. When we started this program, employees paid for their classes up front, and if they got a C, they'd get a certain amount reimbursed; if they got a B or above, they'd be fully reimbursed. We later changed that to be more in line with our principles and paid up front for any employee who took a college class. "With this program, the number of people going to take college classes quadrupled immediately," says Pru, who oversaw it. "If you were living the principle of continuous learning, the company was going to invest in you."

HELP EMPLOYEES DO THEIR CURRENT JOB BETTER—AND PREPARE FOR THEIR NEXT ONE

Continuous learning is nonnegotiable if your employees are going to increase their productivity. In the Society for Human Resource Management's 2022 Workplace Learning & Development Trends survey, 55 percent of workers surveyed said they needed additional training to perform better in their current job role.[5] A 2020 study by the World Economic Forum forecasted that 50 percent of employees will need reskilling by 2025, a trend that is only likely to accelerate as AI continues to infiltrate the workplace.[6] But to sustain long-term growth, it is not enough to equip your employees with the skills they need to succeed in their current jobs. You also need to prepare them for their next ones.

If people can't learn and grow within an organization, they get stressed, they disengage, and they leave. In the APA's 2023 Work in America Survey, 66 percent of workers who said they lacked growth and advancement opportunities felt tense and stressed out during their workday. Among those who were satisfied with their opportunities, only 42 percent felt this way.[7] Similarly, in a 2021 Gallup-Amazon survey of more than 15,000 US workers, 48 percent said they would switch to a new job if it offered better skills-training opportunities.[8]

Our Continuous Learning programs prioritized skills that people needed in their current jobs, while also encouraging them to explore other parts of the business that interested them and to acquire the skills needed to advance or move laterally within the company. Research published in the *MIT Sloan Management Review* found that the opportunity to make a lateral career move was 2.5 times more important than pay in predicting employee retention and 12 times more effective than offering someone a promotion.[9] Employees who are given the opportunity to move to new positions internally— whether moving up or laterally—are also 3.5 times more likely to be engaged.

We worked at improving retention and internal hiring, always aiming to be better and better. Through the 2000s, even as we grew from a few hundred employees to several thousand and as our business changed with the acquisition of Keurig, we improved internal hiring from 11 to 25 percent and enjoyed a retention rate of about 90 percent. In 2009, 93 percent of Green Mountain employees said we were "a great place to work."

MAKE THE BUSINESS EVERYONE'S BUSINESS

Co-creation in business depends on having partners—including employees—who are empowered with an understanding of the company strategy they are trying to support. One of the things I liked about business theorist W. Edwards Deming's approach to continuous improvement was the idea that you should be able to walk around and ask employees to explain what they were doing and how it contributed to the overall mission of the organization. A key part of our Continuous Learning program was teaching the fundamentals of our business, ensuring that every employee understood how we made our product, how we made money, and how inputs at the departmental and the individual level fit in.

Naturally, we offered training about coffee, including a Passion for Coffee course for beginners. There was also a Masters Coffee College—covering everything from coffee origins and growing practices to roasting, processing, and service—for people looking to take their product knowledge further. I wanted employees to understand how every step in handling the beans impacted the flavor and overall quality of what we ultimately delivered to customers.

Through Continuous Learning classes, as well as larger-scale activities, we aimed to make the other fundamentals of our business just as clear for all our employees. We looked for programs that would engage them in high-level thinking about the business and what makes it successful.

One of my favorite trainings was a hands-on exercise in business finance known as the Frac Pack Challenge, which helped show employees, regardless of their level of business sophistication, how all the costs in the "tree-to-cup" journey of our coffee determined our profits. Developed in the early 2000s in conjunction with Praxis Consulting, the training involved taking a case of the "fractional" coffee packs that we manufactured for food service customers. There were 100 packs in each case. People from different areas of the company would get up and explain the work they did at each step of the process, and they'd remove a certain number of packs to represent the relative expense of that step.

For example, paying the coffee farmer $1.15 a pound for green coffee was roughly 20 percent of our sales, so we would remove 20 packs of coffee. Dealing with brokers and shipping coffee to our plant in Waterbury cost another three packs. In the roasting process, you lose about 16 percent of the weight of the coffee, which subtracted more packs. Paying for packaging materials and the cost of running the packaging machines took away still more. Once we'd covered all the expenses of producing coffee, we'd be left with, say, a margin of about 40 percent—or 40 packs of coffee. Then people would talk about the operational expenses of servicing customer accounts—everything from delivery, to our call center, to accounting and data entry—removing more and more frac packs from the case. When everything was accounted for, we'd be left with maybe four or five packs of coffee. For employees who had assumed that what we reported as "revenue" was all money that we got to keep, it was eye-opening to see how few packs were left over. And it really drove home how even little improvements and cost savings in each area of the business could add to our bottom line.

As important as the content of the class was the way that it was taught. When the program was first developed, several senior executives volunteered to teach it; I opted instead to tap middle managers and frontline employees who understood the material and wanted to share it with others. (Senior executives would be there to answer questions as needed.) "Leadership at Every Level" was a core Green Mountain principle. People who were "in the weeds" of our operations, I felt, were the best ones to explain them. Employees also taught or cotaught our Financial Peace course, our Coffee College curriculum, and classes in process improvement, project management, and manufacturing excellence, to name a few. It made sense to have employees become trainers, because in order to teach someone else, you have to know the subject yourself at a deep level. It also gave employees a sense of pride and fulfillment. And when employees heard information coming from their peers, I felt, it would always be more believable and engaging. A whole section of our Continuous Learning catalog offered classes—in subjects like communication and coaching, managing conflict, and running effective meetings—designed to prepare employees for leadership responsibilities in the company.

The frac pack workshops, along with other trainings we offered, like the Great Game of Business, which introduced concepts of open-book management, allowed us to scale financial and business literacy across a fast-growing employee population. With this training under our belts, as an organization we were able to adopt new ways of tracking and improving performance and of letting employees share in our financial success.

In the mid-2000s, we introduced a "balanced scorecard" approach. That meant every functional area of the company—marketing, manufacturing and distribution, etc.—had a scorecard, with goals that managers and their direct reports came up with collaboratively, reporting on their progress weekly or monthly. So, for example, our manufacturing team aimed to reduce rejected single-serve pods on our production line, which could be as many as 10 or 15 of the total. Improving the rejection rate would have a significant impact on revenue, and it required locating and solving problems at the local level. Whether we were trying to improve efficiency in production or in an accounting process, the point was that teams of people who understood our processes were working on improving them. Instead of management dictating what changes we needed to make, we held meetings where everyone contributed solutions. The company adopted the use of a financial scoreboard in 2004 and began departmental tracking of operating profit as a key organizational metric.

In addition to sharing information about our business with employees—information that they could use to help us improve and grow—I wanted them to share directly in the rewards of their efforts. In 2005, we instituted a companywide profit-sharing plan that rewarded groups who exceeded performance goals. And from the time we went public in 1993, we had programs to promote employee stock ownership and held trainings to explain the concept of shared ownership in the business. In 1998, we launched an employee stock purchase plan, a type of employee stock ownership plan, or ESOP.

I always felt the best way to reward performance was to let people share in the value of the organization as a whole. Our stock purchase program allowed employees to allocate some of their paycheck to buy into a fund of company stock, vesting over five years. The idea was that employees should be able to buy in to the business without having to take any cash out of their own pocket. The company made matching contributions, like a pension fund.

Studies show that public companies with stock option plans had 4 percent greater overall compensation than public companies without them.[10] People of color and young parents who participate in ESOPs report substantially higher income, wealth, and access to benefits than peers without these plans.[11] A study by Rutgers University and the Employee Ownership Foundation conducted during the COVID pandemic found that majority-ESOP-owned companies retained four jobs for every one retained by nonemployee-owned companies.[12] They also did better at protecting the health and safety of workers on the job.

For us, sharing profits—and ownership of the company—with everyone at Green Mountain proved to be a uniquely powerful way to instill a broad-ranging commitment to excellence, and reinforced our commitment to valuing all stakeholders in our business, employees first and foremost. And when Green Mountain stock soared in the late 2000s, we minted numerous millionaires, and helped many more workers who had started out running machines in our factory send their kids to college, buy houses, and retire comfortably.

I remember attending a retirement party in the 2000s for an employee who worked in Maine, installing and servicing coffee machines in restaurant accounts. He'd been with us a long time. "I just can't thank you enough for everything you've done for the company," I told him.

He looked at me and said, "I just want to tell *you* that I'm retiring with a million dollars in the bank." No one expected that the guy who installed the machines was right up there with the VPs and other top executives. But he had taken financial literacy training, participated in our stock purchase plan, and did what we always taught people to do. And it really worked for him. It was immensely satisfying to share the rewards of our work together and see what a difference it made in people's lives.

SUPPORT WHOLE-PERSON GROWTH

In addition to supporting skills development and helping people understand how our business worked, I believed it was important to help employees acquire tools for personal excellence and well-being. We offered classes in financial literacy, which for some families were really life changing. If people can't understand their own finances, they won't understand the vastly more complex finances of the company they work for. After trying out various personal-finance education programs, we settled on one called Financial Peace, a 13-week course that taught people to track their spending and implement budgeting "micropractices" that helped them reduce household debt. People would bring their partner or even kids over age 12, so they could learn, too, and participate fully in the family's budget setting.

Time management, goal setting, and productivity were other areas that I wanted to help employees master. In addition to offering Dale Carnegie training and Stephen Covey's 7 *Habits* course, I was eager to share David Allen's Getting Things Done system, which had had a big impact on me. In 2000, I heard that he had done workshops for the senior management of New York Life Insurance and some other big companies. It was fascinating to me that at the senior management level, people wouldn't already have the time management skills that they needed. How could that be?

In reality, Getting Things Done is more than a time management system. It's a way of organizing your mind to reduce clutter, allowing you to track and prioritize goals and commitments, so you can focus on what's most important and apply your energy where it is most effective. It starts with bringing awareness to your day-to-day activities and putting them into categories, along the lines of "things to do when I'm driving around," "things that involve a phone call," "things to research on the internet," "things that inspire and energize me." Learning more efficient ways to take care of "little stuff" can be really helpful in freeing up your time for loftier goals.

I recall a seminar in which David spoke about internal "set points." He used the analogy of a thermostat. If you set the thermostat to 70 degrees, the heating will turn on if the current temperature is too low or if it is cooling down outside. Likewise, if the temperature inside is starting to exceed 70 degrees, the system will switch on the air conditioning. It activates when external reality no longer matches its internal set point. But when it is 70 degrees inside, the system can go on cruise control. In our lives, we get used to being on cruise control, staying at the level that is comfortable for us. Unfortunately, sometimes we all have to push ourselves. Whether the challenge is to show up in a new way at home or at work, you will find it hard to change your internal set point, because you always have to be "on." Luckily, visualization can be a huge help. If you are anxious about waking up on time, maintaining your balance at the bank, or fighting procrastination, try visualizing what success looks like for you. By shifting your set points this way, the new behaviors you want to cultivate will start to become automatic.

I've mentioned previously how we used visualization in meetings to collectively focus on the future we wanted to achieve by, say, imagining a business story that's been written about us 10 years in the future. Through the various self-improvement classes we offered, employees started to apply these techniques in their personal lives: I remember one employee who loved to fish and dreamed of taking a big fishing vacation—he came to work wearing a fishing vest and carrying his net and fly-fishing rod, visualizing the goal in a concrete way!

We had David Allen himself come to Green Mountain at least half a dozen times for daylong and multiday seminars, which presented a breakthrough way of looking at the world for many employees. I was so excited about his concepts that I wanted to share them with as many people as possible. In 2004, we hosted David for a Mastering Workflow seminar that we opened up to the public, with several hundred people attending.[13] We charged a nominal fee to attend, and partnered with local newspapers and radio stations to promote the event in exchange for tickets. We invited many people from local nonprofits and the United Way, as well as some of our vendors in the area. I felt not only was this great advertising and brand development—the event was funded by the Green Mountain Coffee Roasters Foundation—but it reflected our commitment to what I would later identify as an essential element of the Better and Better Blueprint: sharing direct, positive experiences of our brand.

Another course we offered, the Energy Project, was specifically focused on preventing burnout. In the mid-2000s, Green Mountain was growing much faster than the 4 to 5 percent annual growth rate of a normal consumer packaged goods company—it was more like 60 percent a year. Sustaining that took a ton of work. Add to that, we were a purpose-driven organization, where people tend to give even more—and occasionally to overdo it. Participants in the Energy Project took a survey to understand where their energy was going and to identify specific small changes that could help them create a sustainable routine. The participants each then tracked their own outcomes over the next weeks and months. There was one guy in R&D, I remember, who chose to improve his bedtime routine. "That was his micropractice," Pru recalls. He would say, "My kids like me better—they told me. My wife likes me better." He couldn't believe it. You can be sure that changes like that have an impact on how people show up at work, too.

Another course called Your Wildest Dreams focused on life and career planning, helping people figure out what they really wanted. Sometimes, the voyage of self-discovery might even lead to employees realizing they would be happier doing something other than working for Green Mountain. In the early 2000s, a journalist writing about our company's personal-growth programs asked for an example of an employee I was really proud of for his personal growth. Right away, I thought of a guy named Pete, who had worked for us in coffee production. After doing meditation and visualization exercises, Pete decided he didn't want to work at Green Mountain anymore. His real passion was in martial arts. He left the company and followed a longtime dream, starting a martial arts studio a block from our offices in Waterbury, which he ran for 10 years before he moved to New Hampshire and opened a studio there.

As far as I am concerned, that's not money wasted. When you've helped employees find their direction in life, even if they decide to leave, that's a good outcome. When people leave like this, they go on to become ambassadors for your company, and they advocate for you as a place that helps people learn and grow. I think that it also creates stronger engagement and loyalty among employees who stay. For leaders who want to build happy organizations, the ability to orchestrate graceful exits for employees who decide to move on is increasingly recognized as a cultural necessity and vital component of brand reputation.

LEAD WITH MINDFULNESS

Perhaps the most distinctive feature of Green Mountain's culture of learning was our commitment to teaching and practicing various mindfulness techniques, which dates back to the 1990s when we started offering optional multiday classes in the Silva Method. By the mid-2000s, I'd built a corporate meditation room, and we even had a Zen monk lead regular classes on our Waterbury campus. I believe that our focus on cultivating mindfulness was a unique and essential element in our success as a company, and I include it as one of the core Better and Better Blueprint principles that I believe all organizations can benefit from.

Workplace mindfulness training could go a long way toward countering the widespread stress among workers today. According to Gallup's 2023 State of the Global Workforce report, workplace stress is at record highs—44 percent of employees surveyed say they experience stress at work "a lot."[14] Workers overwhelmingly want and expect employers to care about their overall well-being, including mental health. Investing in healthy, happy employees is not just the right thing to do; it is sound business. In the APA's 2023 Work in America Survey, 92 percent of workers said it was very or somewhat important to them to work for an organization that provides support for mental health.[15] Yet in a different Gallup survey of US workers from 2022, only 24 percent strongly agreed with this statement: "My organization cares about my overall well-being." That is the lowest percentage in nearly a decade, and it's a huge miss for leaders, because employees who feel cared for are 69 percent less likely to actively search for a new job than their peers, 71 percent less likely to feel burned out, and five times more likely to promote their company as a good place to work.[16]

Japanese companies such as Panasonic and Toyota have long infused meditation and mindfulness practice into their business management philosophies—mindfulness is the "Zen" in *kaizen*, the lean management concept of continuous improvement. Zen open-mindedness underlies Toyota's employee suggestion system and quality circles.[17] It empowers employees to adopt a "beginner's mind" when approaching work-related problems. But when we introduced workplace mindfulness training, it was widely considered pretty "out there."

In 2004 or thereabouts, I was invited to speak at the annual convention of the National Coffee Association, which had several hundred attendees and was dominated by the biggest players in the industry. I'd been asked to speak because I'd taken Green Mountain from zero to being on the radar of the biggest companies, and I was really nervous. When I got up and told the audience that the reason we grew like we did was our culture and the atmosphere we'd created through meditation, people in the room looked at me like I had been smoking too much of the product associated with my former company. There were certainly people in our company, too, who snickered about the meditation room. But hundreds of people took part in our mindfulness training programs, and most found them rewarding.

In the early 2000s, an American-born ordained Buddhist monk and contemplative science researcher named Shinzen Young came to the company and for several years taught meditation to employees and led weekend workshops that were open to the public. Then in his forties, Shinzen had the shaved head of a monk, but wore jeans, flannels, and down vests like the rest of us. He brought a thoughtful, smiling presence to our Waterbury campus and was enthusiastic about working with employees across the company, in groups and individually. He taught insight meditation and a method called Unified Mindfulness, which used everyday language and concepts to make meditation more accessible to a Western audience.

If Shinzen's meditation was not for you, we also offered classes in yoga, breathwork, or biofeedback. And we continued to offer training in the Silva Method, which had been a big influence on me. Developed in the 1960s by José Silva, a self-taught businessperson, the method includes practices to promote relaxation, improve learning and memory, help with attaining goals, and unlock extraordinary powers of perception.

People who have studied Silva have reported a range of incredible-sounding new abilities, from making parking spots "magically" appear, to intuitively "knowing" the answers on a test, to performing accurate psychic "readings" of distant strangers—describing what they looked like, whether they were sick, and more, based solely on hearing their name. I've had many of these experiences myself. One employee I introduced to the Silva Method even used its healing visualizations to speed his recovery after breaking his arm in a biking accident. Although the doctor told him it would take six weeks to heal, when he returned for an x-ray after three weeks, the doctor couldn't believe he was looking at the correct images—the bone was already completely healed.

A key part of Silva's program is a meditation practice that allows you to sustain an alpha state, where your brainwave frequencies resemble those when you are daydreaming or on the edge of sleep. It's not a higher level of consciousness, but a lower one—at which one is more receptive to things that the fully awake "thinking" mind doesn't usually pick up on. The alpha level is where your creativity happens— think of how often the solution to a nagging problem comes when you're taking a shower, driving, or walking, rather than "thinking about it." That's because intuition takes over. On the alpha level, we can tap into thoughts that would never occur to us in a normal waking state, and summon the psychic resources needed to manifest our goals.

I didn't make anyone study the Silva Method—or any particular approach to mindfulness—but for many friends, colleagues, and employees who did, it was transformative, increasing their capacity to make good things happen in their lives. You didn't have to be a New Age type to get the benefits, either. I recall an early employee, Mike Pelchar, telling me: "I don't believe this stuff, but I have got my house, and all these other things I've dreamt of having. This stuff works."

Mindfulness practice seeded itself in different parts of the organization. Lynne Herbert, a key person in our IT department, recalls how the widespread embrace of meditation in her group enhanced everyday problem solving and collaboration: "Half of our IT group went through a multiday Silva method training," Lynne says. "That was part of our corporate way of working. Throughout my career with the company, I started my team meetings with a five-minute meditation. I still meditate every day. It clears the clutter out of my brain."

Everyone at Green Mountain had access to the same wellness and mindfulness classes. But for some of our employees, we designed additional programs tailored to the particular stresses of their workday. In 2004, Shinzen and an in-house occupational health expert, working collaboratively, designed and implemented a five-minute mindful-stretching practice that all the manufacturing employees were invited to do at the beginning of their shift. We had instructors at all our plants across the country get regularly recertified, promoting a uniform program, which was all about starting your day mindfully. So no matter what happened on the way to work or what it was like getting your kids on the bus, you could take some time to get refocused as you warmed up your body.

I remember Shinzen telling me that meditation is like going to the gym for your mind. In the gym, you build strength, and in time you can do things that you could not do before. With meditation, you develop your mental abilities to attain things that were not possible before. Improving your ability to focus and concentrate helps with everything.

I believe meditation and mindfulness should be taught in all colleges and business schools alongside finance and marketing. People can embrace it or not, but they should certainly understand some basics. It is estimated that more than half of US employers now offer some form of mindfulness training to their workers.[18] Companies like Google, Apple, Salesforce, Nike, and Aetna all tout their mindfulness programs—and their cushy corporate meditation spaces. And there is nothing "fringe" about mindfulness anymore: The benefits of meditation for attention, memory, and executive function have been well documented.[19] A 2022 study in *JAMA Psychiatry* by researchers from Harvard Medical School, New York University Grossman School of Medicine, Georgetown University Medical Center, and others found that a mindfulness-based stress reduction program had roughly the same impact as taking a commonly prescribed antianxiety drug.[20]

While mindfulness programs at any level of an organization can have a powerful ripple effect, I would argue that they are most successful when the more senior people at the organization lead by example. Adaptable leaders take breaks for reflection and make time for human connection, renewal, and self-care. I could not have met the demands of building Green Mountain without the mental tools and psychological grounding I got from my mindfulness practices. In the mid-1990s, I completed a training program and was certified to teach Deepak Chopra's primordial sound meditation method, which uses a mantra, a repeated word or phrase, to focus the mind. If you were looking for me at Green Mountain's sprawling headquarters in the late 1990s, many days you would have found me sitting in the meditation room—30 minutes in the morning, 30 minutes in the evening.

These practices helped me to stay more "in the zone" and attentive. I was more relaxed, less reactive, better able to respond to whatever came up. I had the energy and the resources of the universe to work with. Good leaders don't only present opportunities for employees to enhance their well-being; they also model mindfulness and self-care, preserving their energy—and that of their employees—by lowering the stress level wherever they can.

SUPPORT PEOPLE FINDING
PURPOSE AND CONNECTION

Encouraging and sponsoring activities that bring employees together in nonwork activities is a triple win: good for employees, good for the company, and good for the larger community, too. Social connection in the workplace is a high priority for employees post-COVID, and for younger ones especially. In the 2022 Microsoft Work Trends Report, 84 percent of employees said they were motivated to return to in-person work by the promise of socializing with coworkers, and 85 percent that they wanted to rebuild team bonds.[20] Gallup's annual State of the Global Workforce report has consistently found that employees who agree with the statement "I have a best friend at work" are more likely to consider themselves highly engaged at work than those who don't.[22]

At Green Mountain, I encouraged employees to come together around volunteer projects. Through our CAFÉ (Community Action for Employees) program, all full-time employees could get paid for up to 52 volunteer hours every year. We promoted a number of volunteer opportunities through our Continuous Learning Expos. From the earliest days of the business, I also encouraged employees to pursue any projects that were personally meaningful to them, whether that meant organizing a blood drive, volunteering with Habitat for Humanity, or helping out at a local food bank. Whenever possible, I encouraged them to make it a collective effort—to see if other people in the company were interested in joining them. Not only did that multiply the individual impact; it also got people meaningfully engaged with each other in a nonwork setting.

Today, a large majority of companies support employee volunteering. In the 2022 Chief Executives for Corporate Purpose Giving in Numbers report, 87 percent of companies offered flexible scheduling or paid time off for employees who want to volunteer.[23] Some businesses amplify their employees' volunteer time with additional financial contributions—a great way to align company and employee purpose and values. At health insurer Aetna, for example, after an employee has volunteered at least 20 hours with a charity, the company will donate $300 to the group in the person's name.[24] The software company Workday supports both individual and team volunteer efforts, donating $1,000 a year to any nonprofit where an employee has volunteered for 25 hours, and donating $1,000 per event where five or more coworkers volunteer for 25 hours or more.[25]

In 2004, Green Mountain's then 600 or so full- and part-time employees volunteered more than 1,500 hours with various organizations. In that year, we also launched a companywide volunteer event, partnering with a group called River Cleanup, which became an annual tradition. Every spring or summer, we would haul tires and other trash from the Winooski River close to our Vermont headquarters or from local waters near one of our other facilities. We'd set out in donated canoes, with two people to each boat—pairing up senior management with folks from different parts of the company to create deliberately cross-functional teams. With an inspiring purpose and the whole Green Mountain community engaged, these events always had a catalyzing impact. Similar to our trips to origin countries, the river cleanups—getting wet and muddy together—fostered new, durable work friendships. "It meshed everybody together really well," Paul Comey recalls. "And at the end, when we'd pile up a thousand tires in our parking lot, everybody could see that we were really doing good stuff."

While volunteering has a feel-good benefit, simply promoting "fun stuff" can foster a similar sense of collaboration and friendship. For many people just entering the workforce post-COVID, face-to-face time with colleagues is an occasional thing at best. In a 2022 survey by the International Foundation of Employee Benefit Plans, 74 percent of employers said they offered hybrid work arrangements.[26] And according to a World Economic Forum survey from the same year, 68 percent of employees said they preferred hybrid work.[27] Forging connections in the real world still matters, though. Companies just need to be creative in helping to foster those connections.

Meaningful workplace friendships often start with people doing something that's not strictly work-related. The Vermont-based whiskey maker Whistlepig sends groups of employees, along with visiting customers, on frequent guided fly-fishing trips—learning a new skill together and having a good time outdoors. At Green Mountain, I think that one of the reasons the folks in our IT group worked so well together—in addition to their embrace of mindfulness—was the camaraderie they developed in their mountain-biking "gang." It included our database expert Lynne Herbert, her boss, Jim Prevo, and others who would head out on regular lunchtime rides in the rough, wooded terrain behind our Waterbury headquarters. The group was something that employees created themselves—but it emerged out of the environment we created, where people knew they could and should use time during the day to take care of themselves and connect with others. Supporting opportunities for personal connection shows an appreciation of workers as whole people—not just cogs in a machine. And when the connection is coupled with a sense of mission, the impact on engagement is amplified.

At Green Mountain, we gave employees meaningful work, equipped them with the skills they needed to excel, and cared deeply about their total well-being. We offered a combination of growth opportunities, salary, profit sharing, and benefits—including health coverage with 90 percent of premiums paid by the company—that was virtually unrivaled at a business of our size. Our efforts earned us numerous workplace awards for community service, for our wellness programs, for being a psychologically healthy workplace. I never thought of these benefits as a burden. By taking care of employees as well as we could, we could help them be at their best. We could motivate them to take care of the company—*their* company.

LESSONS TO GO

Promote learning, and let employees choose *what* to learn. If you can't offer a wide array of class options in-house, look to partner with outside organizations and reimburse employees. Find options that are accessible and inclusive.

Anticipate employee needs. What will workers need to do their jobs successfully in the next few years and beyond? What stresses and challenges do they face—in the workplace and beyond—that you can help them to manage more effectively?

Cultivate leadership at every level. Everyone in your company knows something that they can teach others about their job. Look for formal opportunities to let people share their knowledge and expertise publicly. Help employees acquire the communication and presentation skills they need to succeed as learning leaders.

Open the books. Providing employees with meaningful metrics on your business's performance builds trust and provides a basis for clear, satisfying performance-based incentives.

Share ownership. Consider incentives, such as stock ownership plans, purchase programs, and profit sharing, that align employee incentives with those of the company and shareholders.

Walk the walk on mindfulness. Showing employees that you can work hard comes easily for most CEOs—it's more challenging, and highly appreciated, when a leader can also model self-care and mindfulness.

Trust that doing good is good business. Investing time and money into holistic employee development fosters engagement and good-will, helping ensure that even people who leave your organization remain strong ambassadors for your brand.

STUDY WHAT YOU WANT TO GROW

Scaling Culture,
Communication,
and Engagement
Across Your
Organization

I n 2001, *Forbes* named me Entrepreneur of the Year and put me on the cover.[1] The accompanying story, illustrated with a photo of me meditating while sitting on a pile of coffee sacks, labeled us "one of the smartest small companies in America." I was happy for the honor and for the coverage of our business—and, of course, it was nice to be called "smart." But I disagreed with the article's conclusion that Green Mountain was "probably not the growth company it used to be."

At the time the article came out, we'd just experienced a tremendous period of growth. After doubling the size of our plant in 1999, we were able to roast 40,000 pounds of coffee a day. But that barely kept up with customer demand as we grew across all our wholesale channels. In 2001, we had sales of over $95 million, up nearly 14 percent from the prior year. That was already huge by specialty coffee standards. From 2000 to 2001, Green Mountain stock more than doubled, outperforming both Starbucks and Peet's Coffee.

But when it came to future growth, I held an ace in my pocket—in the form of the single-cup brewing system we'd been co-developing with Keurig, which we'd launched with commercial customers in 1998 and which already accounted for about 16 percent of company sales. With a consumer model also in the works, I saw a transformative opportunity to grow our business. To realize this opportunity, we would need to execute as well as or better than we ever had as an organization.

I'd long felt that our ability to execute—working collaboratively to deliver the highest-quality product and service to customers—was our major competitive advantage. But as the company grew—we would hire at a rate of 100 employees per year for much of the 2000s—so did the challenge of staying connected and keeping the organization as a whole "on the same page" with regard to our vision and priorities.

Now, when we needed to be more together than ever, our sense of cohesion and common purpose were being challenged.

The results of our first companywide employee experience survey, in 2001, brought that home for me when I saw that "communication" was an area we needed to improve. People who were used to having a high degree of input felt their voices were no longer being heard; some employees felt blindsided by company initiatives, although we'd promoted them in all the usual ways. As I anticipated our organization growing bigger, more geographically dispersed, and more complex, I sought new ways to help maintain our collaborative company culture.

Conceiving of the company as a living organism, I had always sought ways to ensure that every part knew what was going on across the whole entity. If we were not coordinated as a company—if we were without our "central nervous system"—we would never be healthy. To address this, we became early adopters of digital technology that helped us share critical business information and build stronger relationships among employees and with customers, and we adopted a cross-functional process orientation to redefine work and make it more collaborative, efficient, and effective. But the most important turning point, for me, was embracing the principles and practices of Appreciative Inquiry (AI)—a philosophy and method of whole-system change developed in the 1980s by David Cooperrider and Suresh Srivastva, professors at the Weatherhead School of Management at Case Western Reserve University.[2]

Appreciative Inquiry put what I already believed to be true about engaging everyone around a positive vision into a scientific framework, and its strength-based approach to improvement, which I explain in more detail later in this chapter, resonated with me philosophically. At the same time, I recognized AI as a potentially powerful way to scale these principles at Green Mountain and reach another level of excellence in our company. In the decade to come, AI would allow us to leverage assets across our business like never before, unlock the potential in our people, and stay true to the values we lived by.

LET THE (WHOLE) SYSTEM STUDY ITSELF

My introduction to Appreciative Inquiry came in 2000 when we brought in an organizational consultant to help us with leadership development and with some of the cross-functional process teams that we had created over the past several years (see Chapter 3). The exercises she led put dozens of people at the company in conversation about effective teamwork and what they wanted to achieve together. They helped to improve focus and coordination among these teams and encouraged me to dive deeper into AI.

Appreciative Inquiry can be defined in many ways—as a philosophy, a method, a process, a way of being. Cooperrider and his colleagues have defined Appreciative Inquiry as follows:

> [T]he cooperative co-evolutionary search for the best in people, their organizations, and the world around them. It involves the discovery of what gives *life* to a living system when it is most effective, alive, and constructively capable in economic, ecological, and human terms. AI involves the art and practice of asking unconditional positive questions that strengthen a system's capacity to apprehend, anticipate, and heighten its potential. AI interventions focus on the speed of imagination and innovation instead of the negative, critical, and spiraling diagnoses commonly used in organizations.

They further lay out its five "classic" principles:

1. **The Constructionist Principle: Words create worlds.**
   Reality, as we know it, is a subjective vs. objective state and is socially created through language and conversations.

2. **The Simultaneity Principle: Inquiry creates change.**
   Inquiry is an intervention. The moment we ask a question, we begin to create a change. "The questions we ask are fateful."

3. **The Poetic Principle: We can choose what we study.**
   Teams and organizations, like open books, are endless
   sources of study and learning. What we choose to study
   makes a difference. It describes—even creates—the world
   as we know it.

4. **The Anticipatory Principle: Image inspires action.**
   Human systems move in the direction of their images of
   the future. The more positive and hopeful the image of
   the future, the more positive the present-day action.

5. **The Positive Principle: Positive questions lead to positive
   change.**
   Momentum for small- or large-scale change requires
   large amounts of positive affect and social bonding. This
   momentum is best generated through positive questions
   that amplify the positive core.[3]

A sixth, "emergent" principle Cooperrider and his colleagues
have identified is the Wholeness Principle: "Wholeness brings
out the best in people and organizations. Bringing all stakeholders
together in large group forums stimulates creativity and builds collective capacity." In other words, because all parts of the organization are
interrelated, all parts of the system need to be involved in creating its
future. This is a departure from traditional approaches to institutional
change, where senior management, and perhaps some external consultants, would decide what the changes should be.

Fundamentally, Appreciative Inquiry seeks to identify existing
strengths in individuals and organizations to uncover new possibilities. An AI process typically starts with identifying "high points," the
areas where we are "at our best." This challenges a prevailing mindset
that organizations are problems to be solved and sees them instead as
reservoirs of potential. AI proposes—and I firmly believe—that what
you study grows. If you only study problems, that's what grows; you
just see more and more problems.

Take manufacturing as an example. Rather than trying to understand why a certain process or machine keeps breaking down, what if we were to study the machine that has the highest uptime and we were to really understand what kind of training, maintenance, and practices contribute to that? That's very different. If you are looking to improve customer satisfaction, and you have, say, a 90 percent customer satisfaction level, you'd look at why those 90 percent of customers feel satisfied—not why 10 percent don't.

In the early 2000s, I was certified in Appreciative Inquiry at Case Western along with half a dozen others from Green Mountain. This was a big signal that AI wasn't something I wanted to just delegate to HR—it was something I wanted people from all departments to be involved in. And in 2003, I enlisted David Cooperrider himself to help me bring AI to our organization in a big way.

Starting in 2003—the same year we broke ground on a new 52,000-square-foot warehouse and distribution facility—we held multiple companywide AI summits over the course of several years. These events would typically take place over two or three days, and many were led by Cooperrider and his thoughtful and passionate colleague Judy Rodgers. An AI summit is a highly structured large-group meeting that brings together a whole system of internal and external stakeholders to do concentrated work on planning, designing, and implementing strategic initiatives and solutions.

These events would include up to 200 people from across our organization, along with guests. Each summit was built around a particular theme or question. These could be very specific and functional, like how could we close the books quicker? Or how can we expand with facilities outside of Vermont? Other times, the scope was broader and more open-ended. The first summit brought together 161 employees and 40 business partners, asking them to imagine ways to "Increase Our Positive World Benefit Through Phenomenal Sustainable Growth." I was always thinking big! It can't hurt—science suggests that the mere act of imagining a positive image of the future has an impact on our actions to create that future. It becomes a self-fulfilling prophecy. This is expressed in AI's Anticipatory Principle that "image inspires action."

As Cooperrider showed us, AI summits follow a "4-D" process: Discovery, Dream, Design, and Delivery. The Discovery phase identifies stories and examples of high-point moments. In the Dream phase, small groups envision the future state they want to work toward. In the Design phase, small groups would outline and report the particulars of their plan to get there. And finally, in the Delivery phase, we would all work to figure out how to implement the plan (or, often, plans).

One unique aspect of AI summits is that they are—not surprisingly—inquiry-based. That is, they rely on a Q&A interview format that builds on itself as the participants flow through the 4-D process. So the Discovery phase would start with one-on-one interviews that create an immediate energy in the room. If you have 100 people present, you have 50 interviews going on simultaneously—that's a lot of talking!

For these Discovery conversations, participants would be paired with someone in a different role or department at the company, deliberately creating connections across stakeholder groups. You never knew whom you would be paired with. An accountant might be teamed with an IT specialist, a marketing expert—or even a Green Mountain client. This could be unnerving—especially when, say, the receptionist would get paired with the CEO (this happened!)—but once people got into the "interview" process, any nervousness would quickly disappear.

We would all be given questions to ask our partners. So, for example, if we were trying to improve teamwork within the organization, we'd ask people to reflect on experiences of great teamwork they had had, and then ask about their interactions with other people on that team, how that team was led, what factors made that experience so memorable, and what might have made the team work even better. After one person completed the interview, the person listening would briefly "mirror back" what was just said to check that what was said was understood. Then the participants would switch roles.

This approach may be simple, but there is a genius to it. Every person within the organization contains untold knowledge and strengths; by asking questions, we tapped into a previously unimaginable collective capacity. In these conversations, every stakeholder's experience and perspective matters. It is all good "data" for us to learn from and leverage.

In the Dream phase, people would again go into small groups of a half dozen to share visions of a future that we could move toward. This phase would also use positive question prompts: "If you dream that it is 5 or 10 years from now, what are we doing that is different from today?" "Imagine that we are a billion-dollar company, and we've made all our employees and farmers successful—what does that look like and how did we achieve that?" It was OK if the answers were a bit over the top. They didn't all have to be practical ideas. The point was to get comfortable talking about them together. By this time, the whole room would be buzzing.

In the Design phase, we would go from a vision to a plan for making it a reality. Still in our small groups from the Dream phase, we would ask questions that required more immediate answers: "What steps do we need to take to make these dreams real?" "What skills, systems, and groups need to be developed to move things forward?" The answers to these questions would set up the last phase, Delivery, which extended beyond the limited time set aside for each summit. The aim of Delivery was to actually implement the plans we came up with during Design, and a necessary part of this was communicating those plans to those who didn't attend. We would need their help to realize the ambitious plans we came up with. We hoped we could also get them excited to participate in the next summit.

As we quickly discovered, the AI summits promoted a sense of camaraderie at Green Mountain. Diane Davis, my former assistant, recalls, "Whatever the question was, one of the most important outcomes was the connections, meeting people I wouldn't normally see—people from different buildings, different states."

We were a sprawling company now—with a complex of buildings at our Waterbury headquarters in Vermont and manufacturing and distribution hubs across the country. The only way people from disparate parts of the organization could encounter one another was through an intentional effort, and these structured AI conversations could spark an instant connection. You might find out somebody joined the company for the same reason you did, or you have kids in the same school, or you both love fly fishing.

The stories about Green Mountain "at our best" provided many of the most resonant moments for me. Like the stories about employees helping out that we once shared in our town hall meetings, these "high-point" stories helped us reflect on who we were. One such story was about someone in customer service, who found out that a customer in Florida had never seen fall leaves change color. So on her break, she went outside and gathered a bunch of beautiful orange leaves and mailed them to Florida. The customer was elated and sent a very nice thank you note.

Pru Sullivan, who joined Green Mountain in 2004 to run our continuous learning programs (and who was introduced to you earlier in Chapter 5), remembers a materials planner in the roasting division who shared a story during another summit. He and his wife both worked for Green Mountain and took care of several foster kids, one of whom had horrible dental problems from years of neglect. He needed major dental work, but our company benefits generally covered only employees and direct family members. "But when they went to HR," Pru explains, "they were told, 'We're going to figure out how to pay for it.' Those kinds of stories of fundamental caring for human beings and the human beings that they're caring for, because you have a higher purpose—you have a room full of that. It's magic."

In keeping with AI's Wholeness Principle, the participant list for the summits was diverse by design and inclusive of a cross-section of all our company's stakeholders, including employees, coffee farmers, wholesale customers, suppliers, community members, and so on. Because all parts of the organization are interrelated, all parts of the system also have valuable insights that can help to create its future. This aligns with my long-held belief that engaging more people in a process results in greater creativity, alignment, and engagement—and it reinforces the Better and Better Blueprint principle of valuing all stakeholders.

AI summits offered a radical alternative to traditional, siloed management approaches and provided a robust framework to engage with those on the outskirts of our organization, who could yield unique insights we might not otherwise hear. Given how workplaces have become increasingly virtual in recent years, the lessons we learned at these summits about engaging widely distributed employees have only become more relevant.

One thing I loved about the AI process was that whole-system engagement began before the summit. All the planning and design for the summits was done by a cross-sectional team from across the organization. Representing a microcosm of the organization, the summit-planning team worked on the overall topic, the agenda, and the invitation list.

Like your employees, your vendors and customers will have insights that can enhance your mutual success, if you ask the right questions: "What are your best relationships?" "What makes them work?" "How can we make you more successful?" The AI summits provided a platform where our vendors and customers felt comfortable sharing their experiences, good and bad, without being afraid that they were "burning a bridge." Hearing their "best of" stories—why they chose Green Mountain and chose to stay with us—also inspired us and provided an invaluable perspective on our work.

Coffee farmers would talk about how their lives were made better through our work in their communities. Our provider of coffee flavorings shared how Green Mountain dragged him "kicking and screaming" into the organic flavoring market, which had since become his biggest revenue stream. At a 2005 summit on the topic of customer success, a big software vendor explained that even though Green Mountain wasn't its biggest customer, because of our relationship with the company, when we called, the vendor put everything else aside to serve us first. These stories boosted excitement and motivation and built enthusiasm about finding new and creative ways to work together. We would also bring in people from other companies that used AI to share their success stories.

The engagement and excitement that the summits created was like nothing I'd seen up until then. When I would look around at the summits, the whole room would be buzzing with customers, coffee farmers, and employees from the factory floor talking and figuring out how we could work together better. How often do customers and suppliers get to share their perspectives in this way?

At one point during the first summit, we had 20 or so groups in the Design phase talking through ways we could grow and improve our efficiencies in order to have greater world benefit. Each table was then asked to select someone from the group to go to the front of the room and pitch the group's concept to everyone. No one needed a nudge. Before I knew it, there was a line of people waiting to get up there, many of whom had never spoken with a microphone in front of such a large group. A couple of people brought a friend along for support. They didn't have to do this, and they were nervous. But their excitement overcame their fear.

People left AI summits knowing that they could, and should, propose more ideas. The summits reaffirmed that open discussion was not just tolerated, but encouraged. And because employees generated ideas, they felt a sense of ownership in seeing them through. When people have bought in to an initiative—and importantly, the mission of the company—you don't really need to tell them specifically what to do. They tend to figure it out themselves. I had been perplexed when our employee survey showed that people felt we didn't communicate well. After all, we had a company newsletter, posted notices on bulletin boards, and had company meetings. As we implemented Appreciative Inquiry and involved more people in the company's initiatives, though, employees actually started reading all the information we were putting out, and the "communication issues" dramatically improved.

I remember after our first AI summit, where we had come up with a dozen or so initiatives that everybody wanted to get done, somebody asked, "Well, what do we do with all these things?" One of my senior executives said, "I'll take them." And our employees said, 'No, we don't want to give them to you because we want to make these things happen. And we're afraid that if we give them to you, they're going to be neglected or die." It was encouraging that they were comfortable saying that, and it was a good point. That's how engaged they were.

Perhaps more than ever, employees today want to be involved in decision-making and in co-creating excellence in their organizations. In a 2021 survey on workplace well-being by the American Psychological Association, 48 percent of respondents said that "lack of involvement in decisions" contributed to workplace stress.[4] McKinsey research on the relationship between companies' organizational health and their financial performance during the COVID-19 pandemic showed that businesses exhibiting "healthy, resilient" behaviors—including knowledge sharing and bottom-up innovation—were less likely than "unhealthy" organizations to go bankrupt over the following two years.[5]

My experience confirms for me that the best way for an organization to become "better and better" is by encouraging and enhancing the ability of individuals to collaborate and contribute, regardless of their "level" in the business. Appreciative Inquiry was a powerful tool to engage employees and stakeholders in problem solving, vision, and strategy. With it, we became a more innovative, more adaptable, more resilient organization.

COMMIT TO PRINCIPLES

To build an outstanding culture, you need clear and consistent principles. From the beginning, we had promoted five core beliefs: in coffee, in financial performance, in being a destination workplace, in ethics, and in social responsibility. And in 1997, I'd created a revised "Company Vision" and "Core Values and Beliefs" document. It defined our vision "to be the leading specialty coffee company," with the highest quality and the highest market share, and it listed four core values and beliefs. We would:

1. Set and achieve goals that ensure the ultimate coffee experience for our customers.
2. Provide a supportive environment that fosters teamwork, educational opportunities, and continuous improvement of product, of people, and of processes.
3. Sustain our energy and commitment to the company vision while maintaining a healthy balance between personal and work life.
4. Maintain our commitment to local and global communities and the environment.

But by 2003, our employee surveys and other feedback were telling us that employees wanted more detailed guidelines to help them make decisions across the organization. I saw this as an ideal opportunity to use the AI process to engage the whole system in clarifying and defining its own operating rules.

In our first AI summit that year, participants had proposed 21 projects and created teams to take charge of implementing each one, with every team developing a purpose statement, or "provocative proposition," for its project. We decided to use these statements, collectively, as the starting point for a companywide principles document. And so in the weeks to come, a cross-functional project team of more than 20 employees from every area of the company was assembled. With guidance from David Cooperrider and Judy Rodgers, they would draft our Purpose and Principles document, reflecting both their own experience at Green Mountain and the results of our recent AI summit.

The group presented its working draft at our February 2004 Growth Journey Summit, and we asked summit participants—a group of 90-plus employees and participating business partners—to "kick the tires" on the proposed principles. When did these principles "come to life" for them? How would they use the principles? How could the principles be improved? We looked at other companies' principles and how they used them. Afterward, additional employees joined the Purpose and Principles working group to refine the draft based on feedback from the summit. By April, they had a polished version, defining our purpose and 15 operating principles to a wider audience of employees.

The Better and Better Blueprint principle of "valuing all stakeholders" manifested itself beautifully in the purpose statement they came up with: "To create the ultimate coffee experience from tree to cup, and transform how the world understands the role of business." We had always aspired to conduct ourselves in such a way that everyone we interacted with was better off for having known us. The "ultimate coffee experience" meant that every stakeholder, from coffee farmers to consumers, would benefit from their relationship with us.

We printed a pocket-size handout with the Purpose and Principles, which I still carry in my wallet. The principles are as follows:

- **Ethics: do the right thing.** Integrity is the foundation of all our decisions, actions, and relationships.
- **Passion for coffee: from tree to cup.** We roast great coffees and are committed to ensuring that everyone who encounters Green Mountain coffee has an outstanding coffee experience.
- **Sustainability: pathway to our future.** We use resources wisely and make decisions that take into account the well-being of our people, profit, and the planet.
- **Communication: open dialogue.** In our thriving, healthy organization, we share information, ideas, and successes.
- **Appreciating differences: finding opportunity in conflict.** Opportunity comes from welcoming different opinions and ideas with mutual respect.
- **Continuous learning: for today and tomorrow.** Our competitive strengths come from the continuous improvement in all that we do. We actively seek out and apply best practices.
- **Business success: financial strength.** We deliver steady growth in market share, sales, and profit. Financial strength benefits employees, stockholders, and communities worldwide.

- **Planning and measuring: to understand and improve we focus on integrated planning throughout the organization to align our strategies.** We gain insights into our successes and challenges by measuring and evaluating the results of our actions.
- **Decision-making: at the most effective level.** We make timely, informed, criteria-based decisions aligned with our business goals. Our decisions are made with personal commitment, ownership, and accountability.
- **Personal excellence: strong organizations rely on strong individuals.** We are responsible to do our personal best for ourselves, our coworkers, and our company. Personal excellence is built on a high level of skills, knowledge, self-awareness, self-motivation, and respectful intentions toward all.
- **Leadership: at every level.** We develop leaders that demonstrate a high level of competence, generate trust, and bring out the best in themselves and those around them.
- **Partnerships: success for all.** We collaborate with our partners for mutual benefit. Our relationships are based on respect, honesty, openness, reliability, and trust.
- **Vibrant workplace: a place where you can make a difference in the world.** We create and maintain a culture that fosters teamwork, fun, personal growth, career paths, financial rewards, and a healthy work-life balance.
- **Shared ownership: thinking and acting like owners.** We meet our commitments and appreciate the contributions of each other. We are stewards of our collective resources. We share equitably in our successes.
- **World benefit: creating positive change.** We are a force for good in the world. We celebrate and support the power of businesses and individuals to bring about positive changes, locally and globally.

The validity of these principles came out of the grassroots collaboration, among hundreds of employees, that went into them. They weren't handed down by a small group of executives; they were generated by employees who volunteered and worked enthusiastically to collect and synthesize the input of their peers. One thing I learned from David Allen is that company rules are often created because principles are not clear or trusted. When you know that people believe in shared standards, you do not always have to give them hard rules.[6]

By co-creating the principles, employees at all levels of the company entered into a relationship of mutual commitment, not one of compliance. "Commitment versus compliance" became another mantra at the company, former head of HR Kathy Brooks recalls. When you're committed, you get things done even when they're hard, and you turn problems into opportunities. When something breaks down, you do not blame the people you work with—you find a better way forward together. Crucially, we also made our employees responsible for enforcing the principles. When an employee felt the principles were not being adhered to, the person could advise someone in human resources, who would then have a discussion with the people involved.

Having clear principles and expectations also creates clear choices. If new employees saw no overlap between our principles at Green Mountain and their own, they would know it was not a good fit. But if they saw their own principles embodied in the way we did business, they would know they had found their people. At Green Mountain, we had a big mission: We wanted to be a force for good in the world. We wanted to be a great workplace, not a mediocre one. We wanted to protect the planet and all its people. And we wanted people who signed up to know what they were getting into. We made it clear to our employees that the success of the organization begins with the success of the individual and that their learning and their participation and engagement would lead to our success. If you stayed, you were all in.

LET THE SUMMITS SINK IN

As we got a few summits under our belt as a company, the trust that they engendered got people working and communicating across departments in a new way. We became a collectively more intelligent business.

"Collective intelligence" is the concept that groups solving problems collaboratively benefit from a type of intelligence that does not exist on the individual level. A 2015 study on group performance by researchers from Carnegie Mellon's Tepper School of Business and MIT's Sloan School of Management found that more collectively intelligent groups "communicate more and participate more equally than other groups."[7] They found that collective intelligence (measured by performance on a series of group business management tests) was significantly predicted by how much spoken and written communication took place within the groups, and how equally communication and work contribution were distributed. They note, "Groups in which one or two people dominated the activity were, in general, less collectively intelligent than those in which the activity was more equally spread among group members." That doesn't surprise me. The researchers also found that highly collectively intelligent teams exhibited steady improvement in performance across the series of tests, suggesting that they had an advantage at retaining new information and applying it to their assignments over time.

As people in our organization got acquainted with AI, some of the biggest benefits we saw came when we applied AI methods to our core work. We were able to refine dozens of processes across the organization—as well as defining new ones—that helped us find efficiencies and execute at the highest levels.

By taking a whole-system approach, we found, for example, that increased spending in one department could significantly lower costs in another department. A different time, a cross-functional team undertook the AI-inspired 25 Cent Challenge to reduce operating costs by about a quarter per pound of coffee sold. The ideas the team generated included consolidating purchase orders for all our buying activities, which allowed us to obtain better prices and optimize payables processing, and updating our tracking and delivery logistics, which would help with cash flow. The 25 Cent Challenge was successfully met.

In our onboarding process, we would use AI to ask new employees about their values and vision for themselves and how they overlapped with the Purpose and Principles of the company. We would also ask them what worked well in the hiring process and how we might improve it in the future. In leadership training, we asked employees to reflect on their best experiences with leaders in the past, and then to imagine a future where they were the leaders that people were celebrating. What stories were being told about them?

We changed the employee evaluation to a "performance accelerator," an opportunity to reflect on an employee's past year and vision for the future. To do this, we shifted performance-rating language away from terms like "meets expectations" to "is a valued contributor." During each performance accelerator, we asked employees to imagine that they had a wildly successful year ahead of them and to describe what that looks like and what support they would need to make it happen. Postmortems became after-action reviews, focusing on understanding our successes so that they could be scaled up.

In all our process improvement quests, we asked people to not only recall high points from the past, but to imagine what an ideal procurement, budgeting, or onboarding model would be in the future. This created positive anticipations of those processes' future efficiency and success.

While we could have easily grown into a siloed organization suffocated by its own growth, we redoubled our effort to make people feel connected and valued, with relationships across the organization. The work we did on communication, collaboration, and co-creation—turbocharged by Appreciative Inquiry—gave us a strong foundation for tackling the big changes and opportunities that still lay ahead.

QUESTIONS TO GO:
A STRENGTHS-BASED INQUIRY

Rather than the Lessons to Go that I've offered in other chapters, here I want to encourage you to ask yourself a number of questions inspired by Appreciative Inquiry:

What are the unique strengths, assets, and opportunities my organization has that we can leverage in new ways?

What is the vision of the future I have for this organization? What will success look like one year, two years, ten years from now?

What do we want to be known for in the world?

What milestones have we achieved and what conditions have helped us achieve them that we can scale in the future?

What values give our organization life?

Even as we change and evolve, what core things should we retain and develop, no matter what?

How can we tap into and leverage the collective intelligence within our organization?

What indicators (internally and externally) will let us know that what we are doing is working?

How might some of our current challenges be reframed into opportunities?

What am I most proud of that we have accomplished in the past? What will we be most proud of accomplishing in the future?

7

CATCHING LIGHTNING IN A K-CUP

Seizing Disruptive Opportunities and Managing Their Impact on Culture

• •

Any founder who is serious about growth will likely consider mergers and acquisitions at some point. Successful M&A can help an organization gain competitive advantage and attain economies of scale. But acquiring and integrating another organization comes with significant risks. According to Bain & Co., global M&A activity totaled $3.2 trillion in 2023[1]—yet studies suggest that between 70 and 90 percent of M&A deals fail, with most failing during the integration process.[2] And a significant portion of failed mergers are doomed by culture: In a 2019 survey of executives conducted by McKinsey, 25 percent cite a lack of cultural cohesion and alignment as the primary reason that integration efforts fail.[3]

By any business metric, Green Mountain's acquisition of the appliance maker Keurig, in 2006, was an astounding success—driving exponential growth in revenues and Green Mountain's stock price. For more than 20 years, Green Mountain had grown by selling a commodity product, coffee—differentiating ourselves through the quality of our product, our focus on customer success, and our environmental and social mission. By the early 2000s, we were generating $100 million or so in annual sales—something few other coffee makers had achieved. But the marketplace was as competitive as ever. We parried competition across every line of business—supermarkets, convenience stores, offices, and food service—from Starbucks, Peet's Coffee, and Dunkin' Donuts; from global food and beverage giants including Nestlé, Kraft Foods, and Sara Lee; and from industry stalwarts Maxwell House and Folgers.

But unlike these competitors, since the early 1990s, we had been investing in and developing a "secret weapon." Our acquisition of Waltham, Massachusetts–based Keurig was the culmination of a 13-year quest, during which our two companies worked together to develop a disruptive single-serve coffee system—an appliance that used special coffee "pods"—and to introduce it commercially. It was always my hope to acquire Keurig outright, and when the opportunity arose, I pounced on it. The result was highly caffeinated growth: Between 2006 and 2011, sales of single-serve coffee pods and machines helped propel net sales from $225 million to $2.65 billion, a nearly 12-fold increase. From 2008 to 2011, our stock rose 1,000 percent.

But the union of our two very different businesses—an eco-conscious coffee roaster and a technology-focused appliance maker—was not without challenges. Employees on the Keurig side enjoyed Green Mountain's outstanding benefits and were engaged with our social responsibility efforts. But they could also get impatient with the Green Mountain way of doing things. We spent a lot of time seeking input from employees and other stakeholders; Keurig was used to moving quickly. And while most Green Mountain employees embraced the merger with a degree of excitement, there were those who questioned our change in focus—were we still a coffee company or something else?—and our commitment to sustainability.

Successfully handling a merger and its impact on organization culture, I believe, requires sustaining an opportunity mindset, valuing what all stakeholders bring to the relationship, keeping the focus on co-creating excellence, and never letting go of your organization's commitment to a higher purpose. It's not easy, and there are things I might have done differently. But by sharing what I've learned, I hope to offer insights that may help others do better.

TEST THE WATERS

Given the poor outcomes of mergers and acquisitions, in general, and the likelihood of cultural friction, you have to ask yourself, is it worth it? One way to "de-risk" the decision is by taking an incremental approach, rather than committing everything all at once. By identifying a big opportunity in single-serve coffee before others were interested, we were able to take our time—roughly 14 years passed between our "discovery" of Keurig and our total acquisition of the company—and to develop a strong working relationship between our businesses.

It was Steve Sabol, then Green Mountain's vice president of sales, who brought the Keurig coffee maker concept to my attention. At a food products show in late 1992 or so, Steve met an electrical engineer named John Sylvan, who had developed a prototype of a highly automated brewing system that made one cup of coffee at a time using a premeasured cartridge. Sylvan and his former Colby College roommate, Peter Dragone, who worked at Chiquita, had formed a company and were looking for investors and a coffee industry partner to help them commercialize their concept. Their third cofounder, Dick Sweeney, was an engineer with small-appliance expertise. The company's name, Keurig, was a Dutch word loosely translated as "excellence."

"I liked the concept," Steve recalls. "What really piqued my interest was the complete and total convenience of picking and choosing what you wanted and making it right then and there. No waste. People drink coffee one cup at a time, and not everyone likes the same kind of coffee. Prior to this, in an office, whoever made the coffee dictated what everyone else had to drink." Green Mountain at the time was also adding flavored coffee choices, like hazelnut and French vanilla. The Keurig brewer could deliver those choices and expand the options. Steve recalls, "I also liked the three guys—they were genuine in what they wanted to do, and they put a lot of effort into it."

Of course, they still needed to perfect the machine, figure out how to manufacture it at commercial scale, and develop a manufacturing process for the coffee-filled cartridges. None of that existed yet. The first email Steve shared with me, asking me to take a look at the equipment, read, "It's a sound concept, but difficult to execute."

I agreed with Steve that if it could be made to work as promised, the Keurig system would be a game changer. We were always looking for things to differentiate us from others, whether that was Fair Trade certification, flavored coffees, or the air pots we used in convenience stores. The automated brewing system solved a vexing "last-mile" quality problem—taking "user error" out of the equation by controlling all the factors of water temperature, coffee measurements, and customer mistakes that can prevent consumers from making quality coffee at home. Coffee from the Keurig device would always be fresh. From a strategic perspective, it was the holy grail in the commodity coffee industry: a unique, patent-protected product that set us apart. Nestlé had introduced the Nespresso single-cup brewing system in Europe in the 1980s—but it made small, European-size servings and hadn't made inroads in North America. It would be several years before other manufacturers started bringing similar products to market.

We weren't the only coffee roaster that the Keurig founders approached. Dunkin' Donuts—which actually purchased a prototype to play with—and our old friends at Brooklyn-based Gillies Coffee Company were among several companies that passed on the opportunity to partner with the untested appliance maker. It would be several years before the industry—and even most people within our company—embraced the single-cup brewing paradigm, or fully understood its disruptive potential.

Looking back, I often wonder, why did Green Mountain get this opportunity, beating out bigger, better-equipped competitors? Largely, I think, it comes down to the fact we "got it" before others did. I was receptive to the opportunity and had confidence in Steve Sabol's positive "read" on the founding team. Embracing an opportunity mindset, Steve and I were able to see past the still-shaky current technology to a better, future version. The entire industry was telling Keurig that this would never work—that you couldn't brew coffee this way. But to me, there was too much potential here to dismiss the opportunity. I asked Steve to stick close to Keurig and to see if we could help. Steve didn't really need my encouragement, though—he was totally committed to pursuing this. As I had done with our Environmental Committee back in the 1980s, I got out of his way.

When I approached the Green Mountain board about making an investment, nobody seemed to share my enthusiasm. So with their caution in mind, I scaled back my proposed investment, and in exchange for $150,000, Green Mountain acquired a 1 percent stake in Keurig. That seems minuscule in retrospect, but it was a lot for a company of our size back then.

For a couple of years, we had an "exploratory" relationship with Keurig, sending Green Mountain employees there to help refine the technology, sharing our expertise in grinding, packaging, and brewing. "We worked with them for six months on the coffee grind and the water pressure of the machine until we got it right," recalls Curtis Hooper, who was in charge of coffee quality for our wholesale accounts. "We figured out how we could brew in less time, by adding pressure. Nobody thought you could do that. It was a whole new formula."

As we hit key milestones, Green Mountain's commitment to Keurig grew stronger. In 1994, we entered into a nonexclusive licensing and manufacturing agreement. Under the deal, we set up a prototype manufacturing line at our facility, using machinery provided by Keurig, to produce K-Cups packed with Green Mountain coffee. We weren't going to make a huge investment until we saw a viable manufacturing path.

We had always worked to create the highest-quality product possible. Now, we had to adapt our methods to make something entirely new. Perfecting the grind size was one of the big challenges—it had to be just right to work in the Keurig brewer. In the early 1990s, our ability to control the grind size and shape was more limited, but over time, through a continuous improvement process, we got better and better. When roller grinders came out, we embraced them. The grinders could get hot, though, which started breaking down the coffee and hurting quality, so we switched to more expensive water-cooled grinders. Our safety protocols had to evolve with our new manufacturing technology, too. Grinding coffee beans releases a lot of carbon dioxide, so the grinders were moved into a separate room with its own ventilation equipment and warning signs on the doors.

In 1996, we manufactured branded K-Cups filled with Green Mountain coffee for customer trials in Boston-area offices. Until

Keurig could manufacture a lower-cost consumer machine, the plan for rolling out the product was to focus first on the lucrative office coffee service market.

The trials of the system were a resounding success, and in 1998, we bought the first run of 300 Keurig machines to provide to our office customers and launched commercial sales of Green Mountain K-Cups. In 1999—although we were now competing against so-called portion-pack brewing systems from other manufacturers, as well as a single-serve brewing system similar to the Keurig made by Flavia, a division of US food giant Mars—we doubled the number of distributors we worked with and increased the pounds of coffee sold through the office channel by nearly 40 percent. In fiscal year 2000—two years after their commercial launch—sales of K-Cups made up nearly 16 percent of our total sales, and we signed a 10-year manufacturing and distribution agreement with Keurig.

Keurig's system—and the high margins we enjoyed on coffee sold in K-Cups—was really moving the needle for our business. But competition was intensifying. By 2001, Diedrich Coffee, Procter & Gamble's Millstone brand, and Timothy's were also making licensed K-Cups. In 2002, we made a move to increase our ownership stake at Keurig, buying out 100 or so individual early investors to secure a greater than 50 percent interest in the company. But Keurig's management didn't like that, and in a bit of gamesmanship, Keurig convinced Canadian roaster Van Houtte to buy a stake in the business, which drove our total stake down to 42 percent.

When Keurig finally launched its single-cup brewer for the home in 2003, Procter & Gamble, Sara Lee, Kraft, and Nestlé all quickly followed with their own appliances. Luckily—or rather, by design!—we still enjoyed a first-mover advantage, including considerable brand recognition from being in the office space, and we had a product and manufacturing process that had been thoroughly debugged and was, to my mind, superior in all ways to anyone else's. In 2005, due primarily to increased sales of Keurig single-cup brewers and K-Cups, our consumer channel grew more than 54 percent in dollar sales and 43.9 percent in coffee pounds shipped. By 2006, there were six companies licensed to package their coffee brands in K-Cup pods. Green Mountain was by far the most successful of them—and the only one with a substantial interest in the Keurig platform.

Thanks to our ownership stake, we shared a portion of the licensing revenue from the other coffee makers that were selling K-Cups. But at the same time, we were still paying a royalty to Keurig ourselves—paying for the right to use a platform that we'd invested years in developing and promoting. And because Green Mountain owned less than half of Keurig's total shares—Keurig's venture backers MDT Advisers had the controlling interest in the company—we had less influence over its management than I would have liked. The biggest risk we faced at this point was that Keurig might somehow get away from us.

In 2006, MDT Advisers got a court order to sell its Keurig stake, and again—recalling my last days at E-Z Wider—I found myself in a nerve-racking bidding war. I had no idea who the other bidders were or what they were offering, but I knew if we didn't bid high enough, there would be no second chance, and I was not going to lose. Facing pushback from the board, still, and skepticism from Wall Street pundits, I beat out a slew of competitors to acquire the remainder of Keurig, in May 2006, for just over $104 million.[4]

LET WHAT WORKS, WORK

Often, the reason for acquiring another business is that it does something different (or better) than you do. It adds something new. Appreciating and understanding what that "something" is—and *how* it is different from your existing value proposition—is essential to keeping the innovative spark of your acquisition target alive. Across any organization, I believe that valuing all stakeholders is a key factor in success—and some of the most essential stakeholders in a merger are the employees you are inheriting.

At the time of the merger, some people at Green Mountain had worked with counterparts at Keurig for nearly a decade—perfecting the brewer, refining the K-Cup manufacturing process, and refining the go-to-market strategy. We appreciated the talent, dedication, and specialized skills they brought to our partnership. We also knew that you could hardly find two more different groups of people.

The Green Mountain–Keurig merger brought together "tight" and "loose" cultures, which organizational experts agree can be especially difficult. Amazon's 2017 acquisition of Whole Foods Markets is a good example.[5] In that case, it was the "tight" culture, Amazon, bringing its way of doing things to a looser culture at Whole Foods. Amazon's culture was characterized by precision, efficiency, and a clear hierarchy. Whole Foods employees, accustomed to an egalitarian workplace organized around self-managed teams, bristled at a host of changes that Amazon implemented after the acquisition.[6] A year after the purchase, a group of Whole Foods staffers put out a list of takeover-related grievances and accelerated (ultimately unsuccessful) unionization efforts.[7] The ultimate success of the merger is still a matter of debate.[8]

Most of Keurig's leadership group had technical or military backgrounds. They were serious about discipline, and they were used to working in highly structured environments. Nick Lazaris, Keurig's CEO, a wiry guy with a restless energy, had a degree from MIT and a Harvard MBA. Before Keurig, he'd been the head of the technical staffing division at Boston recruiter Office Specialists. Keurig's lead engineer, Kevin Sullivan, was a fighter jet pilot before taking charge of GE's satellite program. Ian Tinkler, who worked for him, had been on the design team for a Boeing airliner. Keurig's business development lead, Mark Wood, had been a test pilot on an aircraft carrier. You'd think, what the heck are they doing working on a coffee machine?

At Green Mountain, we encouraged exploration, discovery, and learning as you go. We believed in working collectively, often using nontraditional means to solve problems and help grow the business. No one got fired for genuinely trying to do the right thing. The folks at Keurig had a different way of thinking and working that was effective in their business, which was built around developing a highly engineered piece of equipment to very specific parameters. And though the company was small, the staff accomplished that more successfully than anyone else.

Cultural norms at our two companies were different in almost every way. "Acceptable" dress at Green Mountain was more casual than at Keurig, where a more corporate feel prevailed. Even the physical layout of our businesses signaled our different ways of working and connecting: We held companywide meetings in our huge Demeritt gathering hall; Keurig's headquarters in the Boston suburbs had no real central gathering space. The people there often liked to work things out in isolation.

All that said, we didn't need to do everything the same way—we just had to work effectively as partners. Of course, we had one-on-one meetings with members of Keurig's leadership team premerger, discussing how we'd work together going forward. I decided that, at least in the short term, the businesses should operate at arm's length. For the first year after the acquisition of Keurig, it operated as a wholly owned subsidiary of Green Mountain, with its own operational budget and management structure. I believe we tried to retain every Keurig employee who wanted to stay.

The arrangement made it possible for folks at Keurig to continue their style of working, while we both profited from the advantages of a cozier corporate relationship. We could talk freely about internal business issues, because we were all on the same team. Employees could also transfer between the two companies, and the folks at Keurig got the same benefits package, continuous learning opportunities, and stock ownership program as original Green Mountain employees.

Not everyone was in favor of this "soft integration" of Keurig and Green Mountain. "A lot of board members wanted to tell them what to do and stuff them into the Green Mountain Coffee way of doing things," Steve Sabol remembers. But it worked well enough: In our fiscal year 2007—thanks to big gains in revenue from Keurig brewer sales and licensed K-Cups, the elimination of royalties that we paid to Keurig, and a 41 percent increase year over year in shipments of Green Mountain–branded K-Cups—we had a gross profit of just over $131 million, a 60 percent increase over the previous year's $82 million.

Nonetheless, maintaining separate operations took its toll, creating a gulf that could amplify mistrust and misunderstandings. Keurig CEO Nick Lazaris and I had very different personalities, and we each had strong ideas. We were both used to being in charge, and the fact that he reported directly to me after the merger didn't really sit well with him. We'd butt heads occasionally. "It was a little bit like watching Mom and Dad fight at times, when they're trying to put a happy face on it," recalls Lindsey Bolger, our VP of Coffee Sourcing and Excellence. "There was certainly tension in the room when the waters were being tested." There were inefficiencies in duplicating many core functions across both businesses. While it made sense to slow down the business integration process—and helped us avoid screwing up each company's unique culture—after a year, it was clear to me that we needed to become more unified.

BUILD TRUST . . . PATIENTLY

In 2007, Keurig and Green Mountain began integrating systems that we'd previously kept separate, and a new business structure was established. A new corporate group called Green Mountain Coffee Roasters Inc. oversaw two distinct business units: Keurig Inc. focused on coffee makers, and the Specialty Coffee Business Unit, which included Green Mountain Coffee and several other coffee roasters that we acquired after the Keurig acquisition. Scott McCreary became head of coffee, and Nick Lazaris stayed on as head of Keurig.

We kept the sales and marketing divisions separate. Green Mountain focused on selling coffee, Keurig on selling machines. (That created some tension, as each sales force essentially wanted to take over the other.) We decided that corporate functions such as IT, finance, and HR would be "enterprise" services, serving both Green Mountain and Keurig. "We assessed all the existing systems at our coffee division and at Keurig, decided which systems made the most sense to support the future of the integrated company, and then built a multiyear technology road map to consolidate solutions," Lynne

Herbert, our senior director of IT, recalls. The work was complex and took years to complete. During this transition phase, we relied heavily on consultants, which allowed us to scale up and down as needed, rather than having to constantly hire and fire large numbers of employees, which negatively impacts company morale. The plan was to eventually "right-size" a steady-state technology team for the merged company.

"It was challenging work, building the relationships and trust with business leaders at Keurig," Lynne recalls. "I spent a lot of time road tripping to Massachusetts. Because I had great relationships with the marketing and sales leaders at Green Mountain, I felt I was kind of sent as a messenger to the Keurig people. It was a bit like: 'I'm here from the enterprise to help.'"

Working with our counterparts at Keurig to co-create an integration plan helped to alleviate uncertainty and the mistrust that comes with it. It also helped us be better prepared for subsequent acquisitions. In a two-year period from 2008 to 2010, we acquired several coffee roasters that had been Keurig licensees, including the wholesale businesses of Tully's Coffee, Timothy's World Coffee, Diedrich Coffee, and Van Houtte Coffee. "We didn't care if you were a legacy Green Mountain Coffee person or Keurig person or a Tully's person," Lynne remembers. "We immediately were a team trying to execute something. Once our initiatives were locked in, we rarely had problems."

Merging operations and technology platforms didn't magically cause everyone at Keurig to embrace Green Mountain's way of doing things, though. That took time and persistence. We were intentional about introducing Keurig employees to the "Green Mountain way," and made an array of efforts to sell them on our culture. This included frequent trips by informal company "ambassadors" from Green Mountain to meet with Keurig counterparts in Massachusetts. Among those who regularly shuttled between Waterbury and Keurig's Massachusetts headquarters were Steve Sabol, who had worked more closely with Keurig's team than anyone else from Green Mountain; Kathy Brooks, our head of HR; and Mike Dupee, who led our CSR efforts. They tried to build a rapport in person, helping to translate and explain the nuances of our culture for Keurig counterparts who could be skeptical, baffled, or both. "Green Mountain culture was just very different from theirs," says Kathy. People from Keurig also came to Waterbury.

"It was an eight-hour round trip," recalls Mike Dupee, an early warehouse employee who left to go to grad school, worked on Wall Street, and several years later came back to head Green Mountain's CSR efforts. "It was inefficient, but there was a lot of emphasis on try-ing to be with each other, to show up and spread the culture. It was a tougher task to communicate and win hearts and minds over to the Green Mountain culture in the suburbs of Boston, compared to Vermont."

At times, a palpable sense of competition—a lingering internal debate about which company brought more value to the merger—could bubble to the surface. Mike recalls being in a dinner meeting with folks from Keurig senior management when one of them started crowing about how they were served a bigger piece of cake than Mike was. "I didn't really care," Mike remembers. "But I said, in a joking way, 'I didn't realize it was a competition.' The guy from Keurig fired right back, saying, 'Everything is a competition.' And he wasn't jok-ing. I get competing in sports, and competing in the marketplace, for sure. But to feel like competition is more important than collabora-tion inside your own organization, that's exhausting."

On several occasions, we brought everyone from Keurig, plus their families, up to Vermont for our big Employee Appreciation Day, which started with a companywide meeting and then turned into a big, family-oriented fair, complete with rides, games, food, and all kinds of special entertainment—including, once, a sumo wres-tling exhibition. A key factor in our culture of transformative human engagement at Green Mountain was the sharing of positive experi-ences—with employees, consumers, and wholesale partners, among others. And in this time of transition postmerger, it was especially important to share these experiences, in person, with new employees from Keurig whom we hoped to engage in co-creating excellence with us. We wanted the folks from Keurig to get a full Green Mountain experience, to see us "at home," to see what we cared about and how we took care of each other.

More than anything else, though, I feel that it was our commitment to the co-creation of excellence—something that both of our companies were passionate about—that made us more and more unified over time. "The breakthroughs happened when we realized that our mutual success really depended upon better collaboration and cooperation between the two organizations," recalls Lindsey Bolger. "It was really delightful when my team and I began to work more closely with the Keurig engineers, thinking about how we could help curate a better coffee experience with their coffee brewers. Coming in as the coffee experts and collaborating with them on things like next-generation brewer technology and filter-and-cup configuration was really a lot of fun. We began to trust one another enough to open our kimonos and share our lab spaces, and it created some great partnerships and wonderful synergies."

STICK TO PRINCIPLES AND ACKNOWLEDGE INTERNAL ANXIETIES

At the time we merged with Keurig, we had recently codified our Purpose and Principles statement—the product of a massively collaborative process involving employees from across our entire business—and the commitments in those documents were always on our minds. We held ourselves accountable to customers, to stakeholders, and to ourselves, and our standards with regard to our impact on supply chain partners and the environment were high. In 2005, we had published our first corporate social responsibility report, which offered concrete data on the impact of our efforts in sustainability, Fair Trade, and community development in coffee-growing regions. Through our experience with Appreciative Inquiry, I felt that within Green Mountain we were more aligned than ever on what we stood for and wanted to hold onto. But with the acquisition of Keurig, we were faced with the challenge of making a different set of people, with a different shared experience, buy into our values and act on them, too. While we discovered through employee surveys that most Keurig employees liked Green Mountain's benefits and social mission, their leadership often seemed frustrated with things like our CSR efforts that didn't necessarily "move the needle."

Figuring out what "responsible" business practices looked like for an appliance maker versus a coffee company was a complicated process that required a thoughtful approach. We had devoted many years to improving sustainability and human rights throughout our supply chain for coffee, which had earned us a lot of recognition. But Keurig had an entirely different supply chain, which involved a lot of overseas contract manufacturing, particularly in China.

The main tool we had to make sure these suppliers followed what we considered to be ethical practices was to implement a code of conduct, outlining expectations about how they would treat workers. We only worked with companies that met these conditions. They treated their employees well because they wanted to get the same workers coming back, rather than recruit new people seasonally. By focusing on what we did, rather than telling them what they should do, we also got the manufacturers to work with us on things like removing some environmentally unfriendly materials from the appliances.

The cultural divisions we had to navigate were not only between Green Mountain and Keurig employees and executives. Our "all-in" embrace of the K-Cup also caused a rift among old-school Green Mountain folks. As we focused investment and resources into areas and units of the company that could produce a major move up the power curve, it reduced what was available for other units. These parts of the company could feel neglected. While many people in the company appreciated our company's growth, and the soaring value of our stock, some thought we were drifting away from our focus on being a coffee company.

But the "elephant in the room" was the perception of the environmental impact of plastic K-Cups. Consumers and longtime Green Mountain employees questioned how flooding the planet with disposable plastic cups fit in with our longtime commitment to sustainability. As the Keurig brewer grew in popularity, we also faced a flurry of negative media attention focused on the waste stream generated by the nonrecyclable K-Cups. Cities including Berkeley, California, even banned them on environmental grounds.[9] To be sure, pursuing the opportunity in single-serve coffee was a study in trade-offs—a challenge to simultaneously maximize good for our stakeholders and to mitigate potential harms.

During the years we spent developing the single-cup brewing system alongside Keurig, Green Mountain commissioned studies to quantify the environmental impact of the K-Cup system. We commissioned a "life-cycle assessment" study to quantify, as best we could, the full impact of the single-serve packaging, and we used that to determine what we might do to reduce that adverse impact. Mike Dupee recalls, "We all wanted the K-Cup to be 'greener,' but there was no consensus on what our goal should be, or what being greener would mean, technically."

This work also allowed us to compare the total impact of single-serve packaging versus traditional coffee brewing. Traditionally, the biggest consumer of coffee is the sink. If consumers actually brewed and drank all the bagged coffee that they bought at the grocery store, the environmental impact of switching to K-Cups that contained the same amount of coffee would be significant. But if consumers wasted half of each pot of coffee they brewed, and by buying K-Cups they would waste significantly less coffee, the two delivery systems would be much more comparable environmentally. I don't know that we promoted these findings well enough.

The engineering challenges involved in making the K-Cups recyclable or biodegradable were daunting, and it wasn't until 2020 that the company announced a truly recyclable capsule. (Nestlé, whose Nespresso brand was the first to sell single-cup coffee makers, in 1986, needed 26 years to develop a readily available recycling option in the United States.[10]) Lindsey Bolger, our head of coffee excellence, recalls: "I think that as long as we were continuing to work to solve the problem—and we were able to do all the other things as well as, if not better than, anyone else—that helped balance the tension. And the growth of the system inspired us to tackle the sustainability challenge."

Meanwhile, we were already far ahead of any major coffee roaster in working on environmental issues like deforestation and habitat destruction and in advancing social change in some of the most economically challenged parts of the world. And selling lots and lots of coffee meant that we could do even more to promote these causes— and buy a lot more coffee from growers who were committed to sustainable practices. Thanks to sales of K-Cups and brewers, the 5 percent of pretax income that we earmarked for philanthropy would eventually grow to nearly $19 million annually. And by leveraging the K-Cup platform, we were also able to partner with companies such as Newman's Own Organics, in 2002, to massively grow the market for organic and Fair Trade–certified coffee, gaining access to the major warehouse clubs Costco, BJ's, and Sam's Club.

"The appetite of this single-serve beast was insatiable," Lindsey Bolger recalls. "When we showed up in a country like Nicaragua, Guatemala, Mexico, Colombia, Rwanda, or Uganda and said we're going to need 20 percent or 30 percent more coffee next year, I mean, it was like we rode into town with white hats on. It was exciting and gratifying to be the good news story in these communities that were just wrecked with compounding challenges of migration, food insecurity, climate change, economic uncertainty, and civil unrest. Being able to show up and say we're going to pay you more; we're going to help you expand your operation; we're going to get you access to preharvested credit; we're going to fill in gaps in your community services—it was just an extraordinary opportunity for my team and me."

Even if there were aspects of our evolving business that not every employee was crazy about, big picture, I think it was clear that we were continuing to make a difference and fulfill our organization's higher purpose. And in a big way.

CHOOSE THE RIGHT LEADER
FOR THE NEW BUSINESS

It's not uncommon, or unexpected, that the CEO of an acquired company steps down after a merger. Nick wasn't ready to step down at Keurig, and I was happy to have his expertise within our business. At the same time, I wondered if I knew everything I needed to know to run a much larger company.

In discussions with the Green Mountain board, we decided to bring in a board member who'd had billion-dollar company experience to help guide us—and me in particular—to attain the growth we knew was possible in the next several years. One of the board candidates I spoke with was Lawrence Blanford—a tall, neat, IBM type who'd been an executive at Maytag and Philips Consumer Electronics before leading Canadian plastics company Royal Group Technologies.

After interviewing him, it occurred to me that I could simply hire him to run the company, and I'd play a more advisory role. After growing a company for more than three decades, in hindsight, this seems like a pretty brash way to choose a successor—and certainly not how I'd advise anyone to go about handling a leadership change. (I'll talk about that more in Chapter 8.) But at the time, Larry struck me as a good person to execute on the strategies that we'd laid out. I also saw that bringing in someone new might help strengthen the integration of Keurig and Green Mountain, without the burden of my history with Nick. By staying on as chairman, I would continue to have a role in guiding the company.

In May 2007, with approval of the board, Larry took over as president and CEO of Green Mountain Coffee Roasters. Shortly thereafter, he fired Nick. And I began a new, challenging phase of the business, working to defend my legacy and the company's Purpose and Principles, in a very different role.

LESSONS TO GO

Know the risks. Acquiring or merging with another organization will inevitably disrupt business as usual and have an impact on culture. Are you ready for that? Is it worth it?

Prepare internally. Find out what your current employees think about acquiring another business or pursuing a radically new strategy. Do they have concerns? How will you address them?

Assess and acknowledge cultural differences. There are growing pains in any merger. Meeting with counterparts at the other organization beforehand to understand what's most important to their way of working can help you address potential flashpoints. There may be areas you can "agree to disagree" on, too.

Don't mess with success. Recognize that organizations have unique ways of working that serve them. Imposing a particular way of doing things can alienate talent and inhibit innovation at an acquired company.

Co-create. Finding projects to work on together can be one of the best ways to break down cultural barriers. Encourage people to meet up outside work with new colleagues, too.

Share the experience. Show new vendors and stakeholders what you value and how you pursue a higher purpose. Consider a pre-merger "summit" meeting that introduces new colleagues to your culture.

8

SUCCESSION

Handing Off
the Cultural Keys

●●

'm a pretty good tennis player. It's something I started seriously working on when I was in my late twenties. I'd play at 6 a.m. at the Midtown Tennis Club in Manhattan almost every day before work, practicing every aspect of my game. I trained with a tennis pro, who told me that I could be a good club player in three years if I really worked at it, and maybe in five years I could play some local tournaments.

Of course, I didn't believe him and thought I could become that good in half the time. After playing for a couple of years, I joined the West Side Tennis Club in Forest Hills and signed up to play in the club's singles tournament. I entered the B-level tournament for intermediate players, rather than the A tournament. I thought that it would be less pressure—until I found out I was the number one seed. I was flattered the club thought I was that good, but it turned a casual event where no one expected much of me to one where I was supposed to win.

In the tournament, I made it to the quarter finals. And then something strange happened: I choked. I was in good shape and had good technique, and I really wanted to win. But I missed easy winning shots. I played terribly. What happened?

In time, I came to recognize that I had prepared myself physically but not mentally. Despite the practice I had put in, I did not have the confidence that I was that good—and I did not have experience playing high-pressure matches. At the time, I understood that I had blown my chance. But I wasn't ready to work harder at it, and I gave up any future tournament desires.

In the past decades, there has been tons of research in sports psychology and what it takes to develop—and maintain—the mindset that I needed that day. As top professional golfer Padraig Harrington has explained, if his life were on the line in a game of golf, all his preparation would be mental.[1] Someone like him, at the top of his game, knows he has mastered the necessary technical skills. The differentiator, in the end, is the mindset that allows him to execute at his best. Similarly, anyone who has started a business—whether it is a small startup, a medium-size firm, or a huge corporation—most likely has the skills and experience necessary to make decisions in a time of crisis. Whether people succeed or fail largely comes down to their mental game.

When it came time to choose a successor at Green Mountain, I forgot the lesson of the tennis match. My mental game was off when I most needed it to be on. I had not developed a clear vision of what a successful transition would look like, despite the visualization and meditation skills I had cultivated for years. I didn't do enough to understand my successor's way of thinking, help him understand mine, and plan how we could work as a team. I failed to consider how much a new leader could change our company culture and alter the course we were on—which I firmly believed was the right one.

But Green Mountain was growing fast, and I had concerns about running such a big company and managing the workload that came with it. We were adding board members who had leadership experience at companies much larger than us. Had I been more mindful, I would have spent more time and creativity finding a solution that was true to my values, that allowed Green Mountain to continue to thrive and to show the world how a business can drive positive change. I should have read books about the keys to a successful succession—or even just looked for advice online. I should have brought the same curiosity and hunger for research that guided me when I originally bought the company. With the advice in this chapter, and with the Better and Better Blueprint, I hope I can give others the advice I wish I had been given.

. . . .

Leadership succession is one of the biggest challenges in running a business, and it's a common one. Typically, somewhere between 10 and 15 percent of companies replace their CEOs each year,[2] and an estimated one-third to one-half of new chief executives fail within their first 18 months.[3] CEOs taking over from founder-CEOs face an especially tough road: On average, they have shorter tenures and worse financial performance.[4] I think founders tend to have a deeper, longer-term view of an organization, as well as a persistence to make things work that is different from the mindset of a professional CEO. And because founders have such a powerful influence on organization culture, their departure can be particularly disorienting.

There's no shortage of cautionary tales. When former General Electric executive Robert Nardelli became CEO at the Home Depot, succeeding founder-CEO Bernard Marcus, he dramatically overhauled the company, replacing an entrepreneurial culture of innovative product design with one relentlessly focused on cost-cutting. In the process, many employees, customers, and shareholders felt alienated from the company they thought they knew.[5] There are also examples of founder-CEOs who retired—only to come back and "right the ship" when their successor fumbled, such as Steve Jobs at Apple or Howard Schultz at Starbucks. Then, too, there are stories that fall somewhere in between. My friends Ben and Jerry, founders of the fabled ice cream company, had to try out a couple of CEOs before finding a long-term fit.

My successor, Larry Blanford, was personable and well liked by many Green Mountain employees. But looking back, I wonder if he was really the best choice to lead the organization, arriving at a time when the company was already in transition. Once he had taken over as the new CEO, I started to worry that his leadership style—which I considered more "top down" than my own—could put the brakes on innovation and engagement across the company.

Larry recognized many core Green Mountain strengths. As he told me and others at the time, "It's like being handed the keys to a high-performance sports car." But I didn't do as much as I could have to help him understand what made the car run so well and the work that went into maintaining it. As it seemed to me at the time, the company's culture and strategy began to change in some important ways under his leadership.

I underestimated the importance and the challenge of transmitting the essence of a unique culture like Green Mountain's to someone who was coming in from the outside. And I could have worked harder to cultivate a board of directors that was solidly aligned with the way I had grown the company, that believed in our social and environmental mission and in honoring our commitments to stakeholders across the organization. I hope other company founders and leaders can benefit from seeing how things unfolded for me at Green Mountain. I hope these principles will encourage them to plan thoughtfully, with all their stakeholders, to make sure that their integrity and core values endure and their organization flourishes.

MAKE SUCCESSION PLANNING A COLLECTIVE EFFORT—AND DON'T WAIT!

Green Mountain's biggest competitive advantage had long been our ability to leverage the collective intelligence of the organization to grow and improve. Yet when it came to deciding who should run the company after me—or whether it was time to hire a new CEO—I didn't make my usual effort to hear everyone's opinions. Many people questioned what I was doing, but I didn't listen to them. I neglected to value our diverse stakeholders in the succession process and to think hard enough about how my decision would affect them, too.

I made my decision to hire Larry on intuition. I was a little burned out, and he was an experienced leader who was, at the moment, between jobs. I thought it would make my life simpler to work with him to deliver on the plans and strategy that we'd laid out. In practice, I should have known this would require detailed communication—and I did not think about what could go wrong without that communication. Had I imagined that Larry would take the company on such a different path from what I had set out, I would not have hired him. Had Larry been given a clearer sense of what I was looking for, perhaps he would not have taken the job, either.

When I handed over the reins in 2007, Green Mountain was firing on all cylinders. So much so that it was hard to imagine anything stopping our momentum. At the end of 2006, our sales had hit a 40 percent growth rate. We were on track to be a billion-dollar business in a few years, with *Fortune* listing us as one of the fastest-growing small companies in the United States. The same year, our stock was added to the Russell 2000 Index. We had surpassed the $1 million mark in our 5 percent donations to social and environmental initiatives. In 2005, we'd become 100 percent carbon neutral and published our first corporate responsibility report. We had clear strategies for immediate and long-term growth. Why not relax a little and let someone else handle the details of execution?

While Bill Davis later told me that he and other board members were surprised at my suggestion, they considered it. In spring 2007, we had recently brought in a new board member, Mike Mardy, who had been executive VP and CFO of the luggage maker TUMI. Larry brought similar big-company experience, which we needed at the time. After interviewing Larry, they supported the decision to hire him.

Research shows that boards will often defer to long-serving, revered CEOs in their choice of a successor—holding back on reasonable questions and concerns.[6] According to an analysis of corporate boards by leadership advisory firm ghSMART, in almost all failed CEO successions, there are one or more board members who are uneasy about the chosen candidate, but who for some reason hesitate to contradict the consensus or feel that they are not fully heard.[7] To counteract this pattern, good boards selecting a new organizational leader should actively encourage diverse perspectives and seek out divergent views, including those of external experts.

Candidates who are handpicked by an outgoing CEO more often than not disappoint. Stanford professor David F. Larcker's 2022 study of the largest companies run by handpicked successors found that most underperformed the S&P 500.[8] This included GE after Jeff Immelt took over and Microsoft after Steve Ballmer followed Bill Gates. (Tim Cook at Apple is a rare exception.)

Between my initial interview with Larry and the announcement of his hire, in May 2007, just a few months passed. In retrospect, that wasn't enough time to make a fully considered decision. If possible, board governance experts suggest that companies start to plan for a leadership succession three years or more in advance of an expected departure. That provides the necessary time to define the essential qualities needed in a leader, identify and/or develop candidates, reexamine the evolving needs of the business, and reinforce the defining principles and strategies that must be preserved regardless of who might end up being in charge.

In 2004, Green Mountain employees had created the Purpose and Principles statement to guide our work and personal development, but at the board level, we hadn't had much discussion about the "pillars of success" that we wanted to continue to rely on going forward. And I never specifically discussed these pillars with Larry.

TAKE A STEP BACK

I never really took Larry under my wing and introduced him to "my" version of the company culture, nor did I feel he wanted me to. After all, Larry had already managed larger companies, and because of that, I think he believed he knew everything he needed to know to run Green Mountain without input from me or the board.

As I saw Larry in action, my feeling was that he didn't value the collaborative way of working that had gotten Green Mountain to where we were. Our way of doing things would probably have been challenging for almost any outsider to grasp, though—especially someone coming from more traditionally managed companies. "Sometimes making decisions takes a little longer in a participative model, because you have to involve more people," recalls Bob Davis, who served on Green Mountain's board. "But it would have been very difficult to have grown as quickly as Green Mountain did from 2006 to 2012 without the bedrock of participation and ownership and a commitment of all employees at all levels."

I'd always advocated guiding and educating people but still letting them figure out the best ways to do their jobs. I did my best to let Larry do that as CEO, but it was scary for me when it felt like he was going off the playing board. Still, I was not all that sure of myself at the time and thought that perhaps I was wrong about what the company needed. So especially when the changes Larry made were small, I kept my opinions to myself.

Like many company founders, I chose to stay in my role as board chairman after I stepped down as CEO. This is a common transition: According to research by PwC, in 2019 nearly 48 percent of long-serving CEOs who left jobs at the world's largest 2,500 companies either remained as board chair or assumed that role at the time of succession.[9] But when a former "iconic" CEO stays on in a chairman role, the successor tends to struggle. Researchers from Peking and Rice Universities found that when an outgoing CEO remains as board chair, it makes the "early dismissal" of the new CEO 2.42 times more likely.[10]

I tried to stay in my lane. As much as I once needed to be all in when we were building Green Mountain, now I needed to find a new way to participate. It wasn't my job anymore to make the strategic and other operating decisions that Larry was making, and I spent a lot less in-person time at the company. As chairman, I attended board meetings—but not our companywide quarterly meetings. I did not have access to many of the people in the organization. My distance was disorienting for longtime employees, who weren't always sure what kinds of information or concerns they should share with me.

So I didn't notice at first all the ways that Green Mountain was changing under Larry's leadership. But soon enough, it felt to me like we were butting heads over important strategic decisions, decisions that reflected a different understanding of what our company stood for and, I thought, a departure from what had made us successful so far.

FOCUS ON THE CORE OF YOUR BUSINESS

When Larry stepped into the CEO role, one of our main business priorities was figuring out how to work with other brands that wanted to sell K-Cups for the Keurig platform. Everyone wanted to be in the single-cup coffee market now, and the Keurig system was the clear category leader.

I had always viewed the Keurig as a platform to deliver a Green Mountain coffee experience to customers. That's where I wanted our focus to be—selling coffee. To that end, in 2009 and 2010, we acquired the wholesale businesses of several regional coffee roasters that had been Keurig licensees, including Tully's Coffee, Timothy's World Coffee, Diedrich Coffee, and Van Houtte Coffee, which expanded our wholesale reach into new parts of the United States and Canada. That was always part of my plan. These wholly owned brands continued to operate independently, manufacturing K-Cups in their own facilities and distributing them. From a business perspective, selling coffee from any of these brands was as beneficial to us as selling Green Mountain–branded coffee.

But there were other companies that wanted to use Keurig technology and were too big for us to buy. We wanted to work with them, too, rather than having them go to another "private-label" manufacturer. So from 2009 to 2012, Green Mountain signed agreements with companies including Newman's Own Organics, Caribou Coffee, Eight O'Clock, the J.M. Smucker Company (which owned the Millstone, Gourmet Selections, and Folgers brands), Dunkin' Donuts, Starbucks, and Costco's Kirkland brand. For these companies, we would manufacture—and in some cases also distribute—their coffee in K-Cups. We didn't make as much profit on these K-Cup licenses, and they were competitive with our own brands in the marketplace. But by keeping control of manufacturing, we were able to keep an eye on quality and have better margins. By 2010, Keurig was the number one brand in total coffee maker sales in the country by value. Sales of brewers were up 55 percent in 2011 and another 24 percent in 2012.

For me, though, the Keurig platform wasn't about selling machines—we didn't make a lot of money on sales of appliances. The business model relied instead on the razor-razorblade concept. That is, the profit comes in the consumables—in this case, the coffee pods. From that perspective, the most important brand within our company remained Green Mountain Coffee. I also believed that a strong Green Mountain brand would benefit us when our Keurig patents expired and we faced a more competitive marketplace, with everyone able to produce K-Cups equally.

Lindsey Bolger, our VP of coffee sourcing and excellence, shared my position. She recalls: "The fundamental debate was whether people fall in love with an appliance or with an experience. Did we celebrate what is in the cup and promote that, or did we celebrate the delivery system?"

In my opinion, Larry's background in the appliance industry led him to orient a lot of the company's sales and marketing efforts toward promoting Keurig machines. We both should have taken more time to think about our long-term strategy and hired consultants to do an analysis of how different decisions would play out.

Another strategic split emerged over how to handle the expiration of the K-Cup patents. My preference was to transition as many consumers as possible to a new single-cup brewing system that we had been developing, called the Vue. The Vue system could make a larger, higher-quality cup of coffee than the old Keurig system. It was more environmentally friendly and easier to manufacture, and it could make other beverages such as lattes and cappuccinos, too. Most important, it was protected by patents into the early 2020s.

Instead, in 2014, under Larry's successor, Brian Kelley, the company released the Keurig 2.0, a new brewer that was equipped with "digital rights management" technology that made it reject unlicensed pods. It was also incompatible with Keurig's My K-Cups, which allowed consumers to fill and reuse pods with their own ground coffee. Consumers were outraged, and soon the machines were modified to accept My K-Cups, but to keep unlicensed pods "locked out." (It was amazing to see how quickly competitors overcame that technology so their off-brand cups could be used with a Keurig.[11])

By failing to prioritize the experience of existing customers, I felt this approach was going against core Green Mountain's principles of co-creating excellence and valuing all stakeholders. If we were truly focused on delivering the highest-quality coffee experience—the cornerstone of the business—we would have pursued the Vue much more aggressively than we did.

Due to a lack of focus on technical improvements, successive iterations of the Keurig brewer declined in quality. "At some point," Steve Sabol recalls, "the focus for the company became lower cost instead of best quality. We were making lots of money, and we could have stayed with the quality no matter what. When you stray from that, it gives you a predictable outcome."

I believe the pursuit of quality also should have led the company to support more aggressively the innovative Kold system, a countertop machine we developed that used a revolutionary technology to deliver cold, carbonated and noncarbonated beverages without the need for refrigeration or a CO_2 canister. It relied on a K-Cup–like pod filled with beads made from a rock called zeolite, which releases carbon dioxide when it's hit with water. Cooling was achieved through a thermal transfer system. The pods needed no refrigeration, and the system was environmentally friendly in that it eliminated the need to ship cans and bottles of beverages that were mostly water. Ultimately, I imagined we'd have the Kold system for cold beverages, a new machine to filter water, another to make baby formula, and our coffee machines to make hot beverages.

But the Kold product that eventually came out in 2015 was not as fully developed as I would have liked, and I felt that the machines were being introduced too quickly into large markets, rather than through a more deliberate phased rollout. They were on the market for only a year or so before the program was shut down, after the acquisition of Green Mountain by a group of investors led by JAB Holding Company in March 2016 (for $13.9 billion in cash).

I often think of the other companies that looked at the K-Cup machine in the early 1990s. Some had prototypes, but they never thought it would amount to anything and dropped it. We didn't drop it. Instead, we made it work. I think we could have done the same for the Kold. The engineers at Keurig were beyond creative and were resourceful in developing the new machine, but in my opinion, we fell short on execution in bringing it to market.

HOLD TO YOUR HIGHER PURPOSE

From the early days of the Environmental Committee in 1989, and even before, Green Mountain was an organization defined by its commitment to a higher purpose. Our commitment to protect the environment and help coffee growers to thrive was integral to the company's unique value proposition and our sense of identity. I was always advocating for improvements in our supply chain that benefited our partners. Even if some changes added a small expense, the benefits in employee engagement and morale led to more effective systems and better shareholder returns. But as our revenues grew, the 5 percent pretax annual net income that we had donated to charity since 1999 became an awful lot of money—and a tempting target for those in the organization who were cutting costs and needed that money for operations.

Today, the concept of multistakeholder accounting, factoring in the value of sustainability and social considerations, is widely understood. But only a decade ago, it was still hard for many to accept. "Back in 2011 or so, we weren't getting the positive shareholder feedback as much," recalls longtime board member Bill Davis. It was hard to get across that our philanthropy, and our whole philosophy of "doing the right thing" by our partners across the globe, wasn't something we did *because* we were successful—it was something we did to make us more successful.

I believed then—as I believe today—that business can be the greatest force for good that has ever been invented, and that companies can and should be engaged in a purpose beyond just making money. From there, it's a simple fact that companies with a strong culture, where people feel they are part of something bigger, are inevitably the most successful.

Our 5 percent commitment was a big deal to Green Mountain employees. My attitude was that it was "money already spent"—it was a pillar of our pursuit of higher purpose. As long as we were making money, we had always found a way to give. We didn't give up A to get B. But more and more, Steve Sabol recalls, it came to be seen as "a piggy bank." In 2012, for the first time since it was introduced, our annual report made no mention of the 5 percent. Instead, it stated that "we allocate a portion of our profits towards philanthropic efforts." When Brian Kelley took over in November 2012, he revamped the way we calculated CSR spending, including counting the premium we paid for Fair Trade coffee as a "donation." In fact, the higher price customers paid for Fair Trade typically offset the premium going to farmers, delivering the same or higher margins for us than our other coffee. I doubt there was any additional cost to the company. So while the 2014 CSR report stated that nearly 6 percent of pretax dollars went to "sustainability spend," the real percentage spent on social and environmental projects was probably closer to 2.5 percent. That's a lot more money than most other companies were spending, and we were still doing plenty of great things in the world. But the tone had shifted to scaling back Fair Trade spending.

A commitment to personal development was, of course, another cornerstone of our culture, manifested in our extensive continuous education offerings that supported mindfulness and engagement in the workplace and beyond. Yet I didn't communicate to Larry, or to Brian after him, just how important this was. Engagement with our employees and other stakeholders and our continuous pursuit of excellence had kept us executing at a high level. Both of these principles were disappearing. With the new leadership, our meditation room was turned into a new executive office suite. Management stopped sharing certain key metrics with employees that we used to track improvements. Cross-functional "process teams" were downsized. There were no more Appreciative Inquiry summits after I stepped down as CEO.

For socially responsible businesses with progressive employee benefits and work policies, the quest to protect corporate values through leadership or ownership changes presents numerous challenges. Some leaders in the movement have modeled innovative approaches. Before Ben & Jerry's was sold to Unilever in 2000, the company founders negotiated significant agreements intended to preserve the company's values and mission, establishing an independent board of directors empowered to protect and defend brand equity, integrity, and social mission.[12]

Patagonia founder Yvon Chouinard, as the primary owner of a privately held company, had other options to preserve his company's mission in perpetuity. In 2022, rather than selling the company or taking it public, which could have led to a change in its values, the 83-year-old Chouinard gave it away, creating a structure that allows Patagonia to continue operating as a for-profit company with an explicit higher purpose.[13] Chouinard's family donated its voting shares, 2 percent of all the company's stock—valued at about $3 billion—and all decision-making authority to a trust that will oversee the company's mission and values. The other 98 percent of the company's stock was put into a nonprofit called the Holdfast Collective, which "will use every dollar received to fight the environmental crisis, protect nature and biodiversity, and support thriving communities, as quickly as possible."[14] Each year, the money Patagonia makes after reinvesting in the business is to be distributed to the nonprofit.

While neither of these approaches will work for all companies, they are a useful spur for the imagination and a good reminder that formally enshrining your organization's purpose and values—making them "succession-proof"—requires time and thoughtful planning.

KEEP THE BOARD ON BOARD

When there are problems in an organization, they need to be addressed quickly. And when boards do not respond, they can make matters worse. By 2010 or so, I was concerned that the path we were on might be unsustainable—and I didn't feel like I was getting through to the board members. I believed that they were interpreting my concerns as a failure to "let go." In retrospect, we should have hired someone to facilitate board discussion about the company's new direction.

Guiding company leadership on strategic decision-making is not an easy task, and most boards fail to do it. A mere 34 percent of 772 directors surveyed by McKinsey in 2013 agreed that the boards on which they served fully comprehended their companies' strategies. Only 22 percent said their boards were completely aware of how their firms created value, and just 16 percent claimed that their boards had a strong understanding of the dynamics of their firms' industry.[15]

Like companies, boards also develop their own culture that needs to be tended with care and attention. I didn't fully appreciate the value of these critical stakeholders, but they can be a tremendous asset— or liability—to any public company, and to many smaller businesses and nonprofits, too. As the company culture changed, I felt the board dynamics changing, too. For example, our stockholder meetings had long been planned by a committee made up of people from finance, marketing, and other departments—in keeping with my principles of co-creating excellence and valuing all stakeholders. Now, finance and legal alone planned the meetings.

I didn't realize how dangerous they were at first. On the surface, the company still seemed to be coasting along. On the remarkable momentum of the Keurig coffee maker and K-Cup sales, our stock surged 100 percent in 2010. And in spring 2011, *Forbes* made it official: Thanks to my holdings in the company, I was now worth over $1 billion on paper, just as I'd visualized when I put the cover of the *Forbes* 400 issue on my wall some 15 years earlier.[16]

But Green Mountain's stock was coming under attack. At an October 2011 conference for hedge fund managers, Greenlight Capital's David Einhorn presented a 100-plus-slide "takedown" of our company, citing the upcoming expiration of our K-Cup patents in making the case that we had nowhere to go but down.[17] Einhorn took a big short position on our stock, and his alert caused our stock to crater. Just about six months after putting me on the billionaire list, *Forbes* reported that because of my stock losses, I no longer made the cut.

Einhorn's presentation also called attention to an ongoing SEC inquiry into our accounting practices, which had begun in 2010 with questions about the discrepancies in the way we were costing K-Cups. We refiled our financial statements to clarify the numbers, but the invasive and expensive investigation continued through 2014, when the SEC quietly announced it was closing the investigation, having found no wrongdoing.

We might have avoided the investigation altogether—or resolved it more quickly—if we had followed the recommendations of an outside audit that had suggested beefing up our accounting department. At the time, we also needed an outside perspective on our investor relations. Our board was divided over whether we were doing a good enough job communicating with analysts and investors. A few board members agreed with company leadership that we were doing really well, but others of us saw warning signs. So we decided to hire an investor relations firm to do an independent survey and report back to us. The firm's findings confirmed my fears that we were not telling investors enough when they asked us hard questions. I now believe that surveys like this should be done regularly—so they can prevent problems from arising and inform your operations, not just force you to be reactive.

To my mind, the challenges from Einhorn should have been met with a rebuttal. I was furious that we didn't come out and set the record straight and point out flaws in his arguments. I had spent three decades building positive sentiment around our brand, and now, I felt, our reputation was being very publicly tarnished. But the board members tasked with planning a response opted, instead, to say nothing.

Then there was the matter of the SEC investigation. I thought the allegations were baseless. Nonetheless, I knew that we had to take them seriously. I advocated for hiring an A-list law firm with experience in handling these matters—in the same way we had for the acquisition of Keurig. I can't say that it would have made a difference in the outcome, but I would have felt better knowing that we did all we could to defend ourselves.

In May 2012, the company released a quarterly earnings report that lowered the full-year profit forecast by about 6 percent, triggering a 50 percent drop in share price. The drop in Green Mountain's stock price was bad news not only for the company, but for me, personally. I had borrowed cash from Deutsche Bank against my shares in Green Mountain. I never thought the stock was as volatile as it turned out to be, and I wanted to avoid selling large quantities of shares because it could be interpreted by investors as a lack of confidence in the company's future. Borrowing against stockholdings is basically a founder's version of taking out a home equity loan.

Our stock dropped on Thursday, May 3, 2012, following the disappointing quarterly earnings report. Deutsche Bank immediately put in a margin call. A few days later, the bank sold some 5 million of my shares that it was holding as collateral, then worth a little over $125.5 million. I was never informed that the sale violated any SEC rule. But the next day, Tuesday, May 8, I was told by the head of our audit committee that the stock sale had run afoul of a newly instituted company policy on insider stock sales, which forbid selling stock within a certain time period of significant events without prior approval from him. (If I had been more vigilant and consulted my own attorney before supporting this policy, I might have been able to have myself grandfathered to protect this kind of stock borrowing.)

Because I violated Green Mountain policy, the board took a vote to remove me as chairman, stripping me of my corresponding committee duties and pay. I was allowed to serve out the three-year director term I'd been elected to in March. I was devastated and surprised that I didn't get more support from board members whom I had worked with for so many years. Some of them I considered friends, and they hadn't even called me to discuss the vote.

In a crackdown on the reckless corporate behavior that helped fuel the 2008 financial crisis, regulators enacted sweeping reforms, including the 2010 Dodd-Frank Act, a major overhaul of the US financial regulatory system that subjected public companies and their boards to an unprecedented level of oversight. In the same period, proxy advisory services that monitor governance practices gained influence, and the large institutional shareholders that control the majority of publicly traded stock were paying more attention than ever to governance practices. These changes made directors of public companies edgier than usual. They strove to avoid the least appearance of impropriety—and sometimes, perhaps, met minor offenses with maximum penalties.

In the months after my removal as Green Mountain chairman, the short-seller Einhorn continued his attacks on us, and the company's stock lost another 20 percent. But the drop was temporary. Nine months later, our stock was back to two-thirds of its value before Einhorn's initial takedown.

In November 2012, Larry was replaced as CEO by Brian Kelley, a former Coca-Cola executive, who, to my mind, effectively dismantled what remained of Green Mountain's culture. In 2014, the company was renamed Keurig Green Mountain, and over the next year, its stock dropped almost 70 percent. In December 2015, it was sold to an investor group led by JAB Holding, which also owned our former rivals Peet's, Stumptown, and Caribou Coffee. Now, we really were just another coffee company.

After spending so long building a high-performing organization that was as much a community as a company, it was disorienting to see the end come so fast. But I was sustained by the thought of all that we had built and managed to do together. I recalled the remarkable sense of collective achievement, the joy and energy of all the people involved—the high points when our efforts to build the business, to grow as people, and to help our partners and community really came together. And once I'd licked my wounds, I knew I'd be ready for new challenges, giving back and sharing my business principles—the Better and Better Blueprint—in new ways.

LESSONS TO GO

Plan for succession now. Experts advise beginning the succession process three years or more before an anticipated exit.

Don't go it alone. Decisions about choosing a successor—including whom to hire and when and if to make a leadership change—affect everyone in your business. The best decisions involve people from across all parts of the company, as well as external experts, in the process. Engage your board in a plan of action, and work together to define search criteria for the new CEO and how you can onboard the person effectively.

If you stay, back off. Research shows that new CEOs have a higher rate of failure and early dismissal when a long-serving predecessor stays on in a chair role. Letting go is hard. If you stay on the board, creating clear expectations about how you'll work together, who will make decisions, and how you will be involved in the business will help you and your successor value each other and build a strong relationship.

Make a "preservation list." A new CEO brings inevitable changes—and that can be a good thing. But you should clearly communicate if you feel certain parts of your business or key elements of your culture need to remain "untouchable" without a rigorous, open inquiry to verify that they are not working. Consider an annual survey to define what employees value most.

Work the board. Overlook your board of directors at your own risk. Schedule regular time to exchange views with everyone on the board, individually if possible. You want board members who understand what has made the company successful and what will keep it on a path of success.

9

THE JOURNEY CONTINUES

Building Cultures of Transformative Engagement

••

After retiring from the board of Keurig Green Mountain in June 2013, I was ready not only to continue my own personal development—but also to take what I had learned at Green Mountain and apply it more broadly, in philanthropy, startup mentorships, higher education, and advocacy for early childhood development and other causes I cared about. My time leading Green Mountain was an incredible learning journey—a practice field for the ideas and philosophies I have come across and explored. Having tested and refined a set of best practices for transformative engagement—the foundations of the Better and Better Blueprint—my focus now was on ways I could support and help grow people and organizations aimed at creating the kind of positive change I had strived for and seen at Green Mountain.

I recall an analogy that I first heard from Shinzen Young, our meditation instructor at Green Mountain in the early 2000s, when he was talking about learning to be mindful in your daily life. When you're learning to drive a car, he explained, you have to focus on what you're doing—how you're steering, your speed, your braking. You work at learning. Once you truly learn something, though, you can simply focus on where you want to go and what you want to achieve. In life, once you've mastered all the "secondary" skills you need to support yourself, making progress toward your goals becomes more effortless. The important thing becomes having a clear vision.

This chapter explores how many of the Better and Better Blueprint principles–such as sustaining an opportunity mindset, cocreating excellence, valuing all stakeholders, and pursuing a higher purpose, among them—can enhance the culture and optimize the impact of almost any organization. My hope is that I can empower other people, leaders, and organizations to embrace the transformative potential of this approach. I invite you to take the journey with me.

MAKE GIVING A COLLECTIVE EFFORT

Outside of the charitable giving we did at Green Mountain, our family has long supported a range of programs and organizations through philanthropy. In 2010, we formalized the Stiller Family Foundation. As in business, I think that philanthropy is most successful when you can make it a group effort. For me, that meant working with family. My wife, Christine, who has a long history working with organizations including United Way in Vermont and Palm Beach, is our foundation president. She is persistent and skilled in helping people and organizations. Our three children—Jules, David, and Christian—are on the foundation board, and we take turns planning and running our meetings and presenting new organizations to learn about. They have helped focus on income inequality and climate change; among other things, they have ensured that the family and those who work for us are carbon neutral through offsets or other programs. In 2013, we were recognized by the Association of Fundraising Professionals as its Most Outstanding Foundation of the Year. And through our focused efforts, I believe we've gotten better and better since then. I first saw how powerful shared giving could be at Green Mountain, where our 5 percent commitment to charitable giving and our policy of offering time off for volunteer work allowed all employees to experience the satisfaction of helping others—without even taking money out of their pockets. We know from employee surveys that this motivated people to work harder and to find more ways to give back even outside of work hours.

Our family foundation has set a goal of donating about 10 percent annually. As with the 5 percent commitment to charitable work we had at Green Mountain, our idea has been to pick a level of giving that felt sustainable and to stick with it.

SHARPEN FOCUS TO MAXIMIZE IMPACT

Soon after forming the Stiller Family Foundation, we were solicited by so many organizations that it became overwhelming. It became clear that we needed a mission statement to focus our giving. We started with the idea of "helping people help themselves." Our statement lists three core principles:

1. Collaborating positively with others to achieve greater goals
2. Realizing the potential that lies within every person
3. Recognizing every individual's capacity for success

Christine and I were really moved by a seminar during a Forbes Summit on Philanthropy in New York City in 2012 on the importance of early childhood education for a range of life outcomes. Christine and I were struck by the data that was presented, including brain scans showing how a lack of mental stimulation before age five resulted in a lack of brain development that could never be corrected. These children would not do well in school and often ended up in the social service or criminal justice systems. Other data showed how early childhood reading levels predict high school graduation and juvenile incarceration rates.[1] The rate of illiteracy for adult inmates is estimated at 75 percent.[2]

It seemed obvious to us that trying to help people succeed at a young age—as early learners—could have an outsized impact and was the most cost-effective intervention for education. For these reasons, supporting youth and their families has always been a pillar of our foundation. "Having a focus made life much easier," Christine recalls. "If somebody sent a letter requesting us to fund their theater group, for example, we could come back to them and say, 'I understand that the arts are very important, but right now our focus is on early childhood education.'" When you change the trajectory of someone's life early on, you can create a vast societal benefit and economic impact.

In 2013, our foundation announced a $1 million pledge to the King Street Center in Burlington, Vermont, to support its Raise the

Bar Capital Campaign, which would fund construction of a new building and expand skills development and support programs for children and families, many of whom are new American citizens. We have given millions of dollars to the Greater Burlington YMCA and supported Spectrum Youth & Family Services, which offers shelter and programs for people experiencing homelessness and other challenges.

I also remain committed to supporting the work of Fair Trade USA by making donations from our foundation and serving on its board of directors, where I help advise—and learn from—the organization's founder and CEO, Paul Rice.[3] I have also served on several other boards, as do many other former Green Mountain employees, who bring the principles and ways of working we developed to enrich other organizations.

By and large, the Stiller Foundation focuses our giving in Vermont. It's the place where I founded and grew Green Mountain and where Christine and I chose to raise our kids. And because it is such a small state—with a population of well under a million people—and not a very wealthy one, we knew our giving and its impact on other donors would make a noticeable difference here.

TRANSFORM THE WAY THE WORLD UNDERSTANDS BUSINESS

One of our core principles at Green Mountain, embedded in our purpose statement, was "transforming the way the world understands business." Working with Champlain College, helping to develop its leadership and grow its business school, has been a wonderful opportunity to create an institutional legacy honoring some of the principles and beliefs that helped me to be successful in business. Champlain is a private institution in Burlington, founded in 1878, with an enrollment of 2,100 full-time undergraduate students in the 2023–2024 school year. *U.S. News & World Report* ranks the school in the Top 10 Most Innovative Schools in the East, with highly regarded master's programs in cybersecurity, information technology, healthcare administration, and business.

When I met Champlain's president, Dave Finney, in the mid-2000s, the school had recently launched a fund-raising campaign for additional facilities to accommodate growth. Pretty much all the school's money comes from donors in Vermont, and Christine and I chipped in to help bolster that effort, which raised $25 million.

Dave and I soon struck up a friendship, and around 2010, as he set about creating a new strategic plan for the college, I suggested he try using the Appreciative Inquiry process. I introduced him to David Cooperrider at Case Western and his protégé Lindsey Godwin, who helped plan an AI summit, which took place over a few days in 2011. "At that point, we were 300 or 350 employees," Dave Finney recalls. "It was a way for the entire institution to experience an appreciative approach to creating something that we badly needed." And it helped the whole organization coalesce around some big, new goals.

The college also brought on Lindsey, who had helped with the summit and is one of the people most familiar with Appreciative Inquiry principles and practice, as a management professor. "We were looking for a way to really make the business school distinctive," Dave says. "We decided that Appreciative Inquiry would be a cornerstone of our business program. And when Lindsey came, it made it much easier for us to incorporate it across the whole college. It became central to the way the school was run."

In 2012, the Stiller Family Foundation made another, larger gift to the college, which went toward establishing the Robert P. Stiller School of Business and the Cooperrider Center for Appreciative Inquiry, which opened in 2014. Our gift also endowed two business school chairs in positive psychology management theory and Appreciative Inquiry, and created a fund to underwrite Appreciative Inquiry programs to benefit Vermont and regional companies and organizations.

I wanted to help students develop the skills that I found helpful for employees at Green Mountain. Why shouldn't business schools share organizational methodologies like David Allen's Getting Things

Done system? Why not share meditation and mindfulness techniques that can help sustain students in both their studies and their future careers? Why not let them experience the rewards of community volunteering?

The Stiller School's approach to business is defined as "Business Done Better." Its mission is to develop "the strengths, integrity, expertise, and entrepreneurial mindset of aspiring and innovative professionals to create positive change in their lives, workplaces, communities, and the world," which aligns with the principles we found so effective for running Green Mountain. In addition to being a global hub for learning, applying, and amplifying Appreciative Inquiry, the Stiller School is one of about 800 schools globally that have signed on to the PRME (Principles of Responsible Management Education) initiative, a collaboration between the United Nations and business schools that aims to promote responsible management education, ensuring that future leaders have the skills needed to balance economic and socially conscious goals that align with the UN's Sustainable Development Goals.

In keeping with our commitment to making higher education available to all Green Mountain employees—through tuition reimbursement programs and other means—the Stiller Family Foundation has also been a strong supporter of Champlain's single-parent scholarship program. "It has almost always been single mothers," Dave Finney says, "and it has been a truly life-altering scholarship."

BUILD CULTURE EARLY

While Keurig Green Mountain was, in many ways, a special company, I believe that the way we worked and the principles we embraced can be implemented and adapted in virtually any sort of business. At first glance, it would be hard to find a company more different from Green Mountain than AgNovos Bioscience, a medical technology startup working to commercialize a revolutionary approach to treating osteoporosis.

James Howe, MD, the company founder and chief medical officer, is a good friend—we lived in the same neighborhood, and our kids grew up playing together. Jim was an orthopedic surgeon and a professor of orthopedics at the University of Vermont Larner College of Medicine and understood the impact that bone fractures have: Nearly one-quarter of hip fracture patients age 50 and over die in the year following the fracture, and six months after, only 15 percent of patients can walk across a room unaided.[4]

Jim was passionate about bringing his procedure—which replaces diseased bone with a cementlike bone filler that actually becomes new bone—to millions of patients in need. But he hadn't yet persuaded the medical companies he'd met with to make an investment. I saw an opportunity that could be bigger than Green Mountain Coffee and could make a real positive difference in the world. But I wanted to better understand what we were getting into.

Jim's son Tanner pulled some numbers together and roughed out a business plan as a favor to his dad. Tanner at the time was a vice president of strategic development and treasury at the amusement park operator Six Flags and had great business experience and connections worldwide. In a short time, he realized we were looking at a major business with significant earning potential. We commissioned McKinsey & Company to do a study on the opportunity and the key issues involved. Encouraged, we launched the business in 2012, and Tanner came in to run the new company. I agreed to be the company's chairman and became an informal mentor to Tanner.

He had never run a medical technology business. "When I arrived, I was very much thinking about the nuts and bolts," Tanner recalls. "What do we have to do? What are the tasks we have to get done?" I encouraged Tanner to focus more on how he would get things done, and on building a culture that would support the company's audacious goals.

"The idea that we'd be building this culture of people who like each other, where we're both considerate and assertive, was really important," Tanner recalls. This was a bit different than what he'd learned in earlier work environments, including the military and private equity firms. "The key," Tanner explains, "was having a strengths orientation, a learning orientation, striving for personal excellence and being engaged with the vision of the business." To that end, I urged Tanner to formulate a vision and guiding principles that would help sustain engagement over the long term—because getting a product to market was going to be a years-long effort.

These principles were defined, in part, through an Appreciative Inquiry summit that included about 80 people, the vast majority of whom were stakeholders from outside the company. The core values principles they ultimately came up with were total innovation, ownership, and tenacity. "We basically are here to extend grandmothers' lives so that they can hang out with their grandchildren," Tanner says. "If people buy into that as an idea, they're in the right place."

Defining values from the get-go, and investing in building culture early, has paid off. It has helped the company make the right hires—people who align with the company's missions and values—and allowed it to weather changes in focus as the company has shifted from R&D to running and completing clinical trials. Tanner has really embraced the idea of continuous improvement in processes that I promoted at Green Mountain, adapting concepts from Appreciative Inquiry, Getting Things Done, and positive psychology in ways that feel natural and productive for him and his employees. An on-site mindfulness room and instruction in yoga and time management systems are key components of the company's benefits. Employees are encouraged to define and work toward learning goals, with the aim of promoting from within as much as possible. Regular employee surveys based on Gallup's Q12 Employee Engagement Survey help Tanner to monitor the cultural pulse and make course corrections as needed.

Tanner comes from a world of high achievers, where the conditions of work can sometimes feel toxic. But it doesn't need to be that way. "A lot of behaviors around achievement don't keep the whole person healthy, and you wind up with either health issues or absenteeism or quitting or unhappiness," Tanner says. "The kind of stuff that Bob taught me can be misinterpreted as 'going easy' on people. But really, when a skills and learning orientation is applied in a culture of achievement—where you're trying to achieve the big hairy audacious goals and people are accountable—it works. And we were very lucky to start at the very beginning."

EMBRACE AN OPPORTUNITY MINDSET TO MANIFEST CHANGE

The call to "start at the very beginning" also holds tremendous meaning for me, in an entirely different context. One of the most satisfying projects I have been able to help with has been the successful effort to increase access to childcare in the state of Vermont, which involved more than a decade of hard work and collaboration with a broad coalition of partners and stakeholders. By thinking in new ways about how to achieve meaningful change, our family foundation was able to take our longtime interest in helping children and families to another level, and to help model a new kind of philanthropy that focuses on making long-term changes through legislative action, working with the nonprofit Let's Grow Kids.

The National Forum on Early Childhood Policy and Programs has estimated that each dollar invested in early childcare yields $4 to $9 in benefits to society. It has always surprised me with all this research showing the benefits that more states have not embraced an approach that prioritizes these investments. In business, the management scholar W. Edwards Deming emphasized fixing quality problems at the source, because it is much more costly to fix things later on. But rather than promoting quality early childcare and early education, society invests too much in later development, when studies show that educational interventions are much less effective.[5]

We felt that given the small size of Vermont, we could show the country and the world what a positive impact a good childcare system has on the economy. In terms of early childhood care, Vermont had major challenges—in a state where 5,000 kids are born each year, about 8,700 children ages zero to five needed childcare but couldn't get access to it because there were no openings. Families who could find childcare were often paying 30 to 40 percent of their household income for it—more than a mortgage. On the flip side, early educators in the state made on average $14 an hour, without benefits. Fast-food jobs were paying higher wages. Childcare was not accessible or affordable, and the business model was so broken that there were no incentives to go into it. Without a comprehensive childcare system that met the needs of all Vermonters, parents couldn't reenter the workforce, employers couldn't fill open positions, families were leaving Vermont, and the state's economy was in decline.

This wasn't a problem you could just put a Band-Aid on. It is traditional for philanthropists to support "direct-service" organizations—groups that fill in a gap or supplement existing resources by providing, say, reading programs, food, housing, or other supports to a particular population. A lot of people like that because you get a note from the recipients, thanking you for making their life a little bit better.

"That brings instant gratification and zero transformational effect," says Aly Richards, who became CEO of Let's Grow Kids in 2015. A former deputy chief of staff for Vermont governor Peter Shumlin, Aly was hired by Let's Grow Kids founder, Rick Davis, to help the organization execute on a new vision and approach to advance equity, affordability, and quality in the childcare system.

Their "three Ps" strategy would focus on policy change, people power, and program innovation. The big idea: Instead of patching holes in the existing, broken childcare system, Let's Grow Kids would mobilize people and politicians to demand legislative solutions that permanently fix the system.

The Vermont state legislature was already moving in the right direction, having passed a historic bill guaranteeing universal pre-K education for three- and four-year-olds in the state in 2014. "If we collaborated, pooled our resources, and focused on a policy solution, we could serve kids and families in perpetuity," Aly recalls. "We've been working on early childhood issues from a philanthropic perspective for decades, and it hasn't actually moved the needle on the systemic, root issues. This was sort of like, let's stop nibbling around the edges."

Working for legislative change would be a long road, though, requiring a sustained financial commitment, long-term vision, and courage. "Many nonprofits traditionally have a huge trepidation around lobbying and advocacy," Aly explains. "There's a lot of aversion to actually going into politics." To get the ball rolling, in 2015, our family foundation committed to giving Let's Grow Kids $20 million over 10 years—$2 million a year. Our gift more than doubled the $17.25 million that the organization had raised through 2014. And it catalyzed further giving that fully funded Let's Grow Kids with flexible capital to accomplish its mission by a target date of 2025. As of June 2023, nearly 1,400 donors had contributed over $56 million to the Let's Grow Kids campaign, including the final $12 million from our initial $20 million gift.

INVEST IN LEADERS AND ORGANIZATIONAL CAPACITY

If you are interested in making a lasting impact on society, I don't think it's enough to just throw money at a cause and hope for the best. With Let's Grow Kids, I was equally focused on developing the organization and its leadership. At Green Mountain, I believed that investing in people's professional skills and personal well-being would always result in better outcomes—for the person and the company. I recognized that the Let's Grow Kids brand-new CEO, Aly Richards, was being asked to deliver on an ambitious agenda. Although she was an accomplished professional—she had led the push to establish Vermont's universal pre-K program while in the governor's office—heading a socially driven nonprofit brought new challenges. Because she brought so many strengths to the organization, I didn't want to see her burn out, personally or professionally.

As I had done in the early days of Green Mountain, I offered book recommendations. "Literally, my bedside table reading was Bob's reading list," Aly recalls. I also made sure that from day one on the job, she had access to regular executive coaching with one of my own trusted advisors, Judy Rodgers. They have spoken by phone for an hour every month for about eight years. "Within a couple minutes she would just understand: what were the challenges I was facing, who were the people, what were the dynamics?" Aly says. "It helped reinforce my own instincts."

"Coaching helped me to be a functional leader in a stressful space," Aly says. "I was a person who could easily burn myself into the ground physically and mentally if I didn't protect against that. I became a mom of twins. COVID was happening, I was running an organization with this serious mission, and I was really in some dire straits. My body broke down. But by embracing a routine of meditation and mindfulness, I was able to be healthy and function as a leader in these last three critical years. I've tried to support my team in doing this, too."

The relationship that we have cultivated with Aly is a good example of co-creation in the context of impact-focused philanthropy. And I can only recommend that all leaders embrace the lessons on mindfulness, self-care, and resilience that she has come to embrace and model so successfully.

ENGAGE ALL YOUR STAKEHOLDERS

Achieving a historic public investment in Vermont's childcare system would require engaging a diverse group of stakeholders to identify priorities, shape strategy, and coordinate resources. In 2017, drawing upon the resources of the new Cooperrider Center for Appreciative Inquiry at Champlain College, we held a two-day Appreciative Inquiry summit that brought together all key stakeholders in the childcare initiative—parents, early educators, nonprofits, business partners, and state agencies working in health, education, and early care and learning. The goal was to explore and develop recommendations for a comprehensive integrated early care and learning system, which would be developed into proposed legislation to deliver to the state legislature by January 2019.

As with the summits we held at Green Mountain, a lot of important work took place before the summit began. This included training teams that would be leading the summit. And because many early childhood stakeholders would be unable to participate in a two-day summit, the coalition partnered with several other early childhood organizations in a community outreach process over the summer of 2017. They conducted 94 one-on-one and group interviews with over 300 early childhood stakeholders—including 31 percent who were parents of children five or under and 19 percent who were early care and learning professionals—in every Vermont county. These interviews captured a vision for the future of Vermont's early care and learning system, and laid the foundation for the two-day in-person summit in October 2017 in which more than 200 people participated.

Building on the information gathered in pre-summit interviews, summit participants outlined a collective vision of the system we wanted in the future and created a deployment document outlining key aspects of their design, including next steps. The final summit report was taken up by a smaller group of stakeholders with policy and implementation expertise, who met in early 2018 to create a draft legislative blueprint, which was presented for feedback that summer. The group sent a final proposal to the legislature in 2019.

"The summit led to some of the key principles that governed the policy work over the next several years," Aly recalls. "It was another big step that really instilled this cross-sector, grassroots, hear-from-many-voices philosophy into the movement at a key time." Ultimately, over 40,000 Vermonters, roughly 5 percent of the state's population, were actively involved in the campaign, demanding change, telling their stories, and influencing what happened and how the policy was crafted.

EVOLVE YOUR TACTICS

Sustaining an opportunity mindset is a key to success in business—and to bringing about real societal change. As we approached the five-year anniversary of our original gift to Let's Grow Kids, I saw that our campaign was at an important inflection point. As a 501(c)(3) organization, Let's Grow Kids could offer education on early childhood issues and advocate for children and families in a general way. But in early 2021, moving into a new legislative season, and leading up to the highly anticipated November 2022 elections, there was an opportunity for more focused political action to get the Vermont Child Care Campaign across the finish line. That required setting up a 501(c)(4) advocacy organization, the Let's Grow Kids Action Network, that would focus on passing laws that fund and sustain a high-quality, affordable childcare system.

This was very unusual for a nonprofit at the time—but we needed the 501(c)(4) for compliance reasons, and to create an umbrella for political action committees to raise additional money. Because it's a less-trodden path in the world of philanthropy, would-be donors were nervous to jump in. But once we committed an initial $750,000 to get the 501(c)(4) started, "it gave permission to other funders to follow suit," Aly says.

In September 2021, the Vermont legislature passed H. 171/Act 45, which laid a foundation for the comprehensive childcare access law we ultimately wanted to pass, and created an immediate $12.7 million budget to stabilize the state's early childhood education system. During the legislative session leading up to the vote, supporters made more than 3,500 contacts with legislators, largely driven by Let's Grow Kids' advocacy efforts. In September 2022, Let's Grow Kids endorsed a slate of 130 candidates in state and federal elections who had committed to prioritizing and increasing public investment in childcare, including US representative Becca Balint, Republican governor Phil Scott, and 123 candidates running for the Vermont House and Senate, representing all parties in state government. In the November elections, 117 of these candidates won, sending the first-ever coalition of self-described childcare champions to the state capitol, including 65 women and 6 people of color, bringing the most women and the most people of color ever into Vermont's General Assembly.[6]

"We were able to be a major player in this last election, which I think was the final piece of the puzzle to get this policy passed," Aly says. "We elevated the issue of childcare so that candidates were always hearing about it from constituents. And promises were made that had to be followed through on during the legislative session."

Finally, in May 2023—a couple of years before the 2025 deadline we'd given ourselves—the Vermont legislature passed the 2023 Child Care Bill (Act 76). In early June, though, the governor vetoed it. But several weeks later, a multipartisan vote of Democrats, Progressives, Republicans, independents, and a libertarian overrode the governor's veto to make it law. Act 76 is the most expansive childcare policy in the country, infusing $125 million annually into Vermont's childcare system. It expands eligibility for the state's childcare financial assistance program so that by the end of 2024, families earning up to 575 percent of the federal poverty level can get some level of aid. That will help make childcare affordable for more than 7,000 additional Vermont families, and more families will qualify for 100 percent financial assistance. Childcare programs will also get state funds to update facilities, compensate staff, improve programs, and boost the number of childcare slots available. The law also addresses gaps in support for children with special needs who are enrolled in childcare programs.

"I think we have really built a better mousetrap for social change, and I hope others pick up on this model," Aly says. "We didn't just pass the largest per capita investment for childcare in the country, or most expansively increase tuition reimbursement rates. We also showed serious political buy-in from all parties, which is really helpful not just in Vermont, but across the nation." Along with our financial support, I am happy and proud that the concepts and tools I shared from my time at Green Mountain provided foundational support for a cause that means so much to me and Christine. And I hope that our innovative approach will inspire others.

· · · · · · ·

The American psychologist Abraham Maslow is perhaps best known for his "hierarchy of needs," which describes five fundamental desires that people need to feel satisfied. Starting from the most basic, these include physiological needs—food, water, shelter, and clothing—followed, in ascending order, by the need for safety, for love and belonging, for esteem, and for self-actualization.[7]

Late in his life, though, Maslow added another level, at the very top of the pyramid, which he called "self-transcendence." While self-actualization refers to realizing one's full potential as an individual—an idea that I had long embraced and had strived for through meditation, continuous learning, and other practices—"self-transcendence" means rising above personal concerns to a higher perspective, which often manifests in a strong desire to help others.[8]

I've observed a similar shift in my thinking, and my priorities—which is part of the impetus behind working on this book. My highest aspiration now doesn't concern becoming "better and better" as an individual, but rather looking toward ways to lift up and enlighten others. We all deserve to have fulfilling lives, work that matters, and fair rewards for our efforts. I hope that by sharing these examples of the work I have continued to support as a retired founder, it will inspire others to share their success for the benefit of others; to pursue innovation and opportunity not just to attain material success, but to pay it forward; to donate, to participate, and to make their communities and the world better and better.

LESSONS TO GO

Promote a culture of giving. Giving is more effective as a collective activity. Within a business, charitable giving with employee input and compensated time off for volunteering are great ways to share the positive psychological impact of giving, with a low "cost of entry" for participants.

Make a commitment to giving. Everyone can give something. Start with small donations that you can sustain. If you can't donate money, give time.

Pick a lane. What charitable and social causes interest you most? Focusing on a particular area makes it easier to become an expert, helping you make more informed donations and increasing your influence in circles you care about.

Talk about it. Publicizing the causes you're donating to or volunteering for may seem like showing off, but setting an example can help promote a broader culture of philanthropy—and perhaps a spirit of friendly competition that ultimately benefits donation recipients.

Help leaders and organizations grow. Offering mentorship and professional resources can help support a resilient culture within nonprofit organizations.

Adopt innovative tactics. Entrepreneurs are used to taking bold risks. Bring the same opportunity mindset to social impact work. Ask yourself: What are the best available tools for achieving your goals? Is it time to try something new? Jump in. Be inventive. Try out new approaches, and do all you can to make this world better and better.

ACKNOWLEDGMENTS

L et me begin with a thank you to the people who inspired me to write this book. It would never have happened without your continued encouragement. My wife, Christine, and our children witnessed the energy and passion of the employees and stakeholders of Green Mountain Coffee and felt it was important to share that history.

Dan Cox, one of Green Mountain's first employees, also insisted that the Green Mountain story needed to be told, to recount how our company changed the coffee industry in the United States in so many ways—from popularizing single-serve coffee to influencing the Specialty Coffee Association, the Fair Trade movement, and other socially responsibility initiatives.

My deepest thanks to Judy Rodgers. I have worked with Judy for over 20 years, and she has supported me as well as coaching others in related ventures. Her help and support were essential to bringing this book together. She felt our culture of engagement and purpose was a timely example for business today. We reflected on different approaches for a couple of years and ultimately found Todd Shuster at the literary agency Aevitas, who with his team brought great energy to this project. A very special thank-you to Adam Bluestein, for diving into the people's stories and helping me find my voice. Lindsey Godwin offered critical insights on the appreciative approach and helped articulate the book's blueprint. And Victoria Pollack has been a great help in bringing these principles to a wider audience.

I want to thank the consultants I worked with over the years who helped guide and educate me. Sue Jamieson and Agnes Cook got us started in human-resource development and Dale Carnegie training for our employees. Getting introduced to Appreciative Inquiry and working with David Cooperrider was a high point of my career, and I value his friendship. Working with David Allen, creator of the Getting Things Done system, was another peak experience. His wisdom helped me personally, and benefited all the organizations I have been involved with. I still occasionally grab his book *Ready for Anything* when I need insights. I want to thank Deepak Chopra, as well. His books and seminars guided my journey, particularly his *The Seven Spiritual Laws of Success*, which I have been referring to for decades.

I am grateful to Shinzen Young for 20-plus years of friendship and for guiding me in my meditation and mindfulness practice. He introduced many of our employees to meditation, helped develop stretching and yoga routines for the workplace, and was very helpful to my son Christian, who is a cofounder and CEO of the Brightmind meditation app. I feel it is one of the best instructional and supportive meditation apps around, and I use it daily.

I would like to offer a special thanks to all the employees and stakeholders of Green Mountain Coffee and Keurig, whose commitment to personal and organizational growth—and to our higher purpose—drove our success and helped to make the world a better place. These include Diane Davis, my assistant for many years, and Steve Sabol, who found and supported the opportunity with Keurig, among other accomplishments. A list of employees who played an invaluable part in our success must also include Paul Comey, Lindsey Bolger, Curtis Hooper, Mike Pelchar, Nancy Metivier, Patty Vincent, Rick Peyser, Don Holly, Pru Sullivan, Kathy Brooks, Agnes Cook, Mike Dupee, Chris Howe, Don Barbario, Alice Canton, Winston Rost, Dave Tilgner and Lori Tilgner, Jim Prevo, Rod Ely, T. J. Whalen, Jim Travis, Scott McCreary, Jon Wettstein, Fran Rathke, Steve Ferreira, Bob Britt, and of course, Doug and Jamie Balne. A special thank you to our board members, including Bill Davis for his longtime support, and Barbara Carlini, who also helped me with insights regarding AgNovos Bioscience. From Keurig, I would like to Nick Lazaris for his leadership—and Chris Stevens, Kevin Sullivan, Ian Tinkler, John Whoriskey, Mike Degnan, Mark Wood, and Dick Sweeney for starting and sticking with the dream.

I have great admiration for Paul Rice and his work on Fair Trade, and all the others who worked with us to implement high standards to improve the lives of the millions of coffee farmers and their families.

I also want to acknowledge and thank Steve Magowan, who has guided and supported my family for many years; Roberta Baskin, for her consult; and Dave Finney, for his advice and for helping get the Stiller School of Business established.

I am remembering my father, Paul Stiller, for being there for me, grounding me with his guidance and business insights, and giving me my first job at Still-Man Manufacturing. I am also fondly recalling my sister Joy and her family. I am thinking, as well, about people I have since lost touch with, including Jane and Burton from the E-Z Wider days.

In reflection, it has been a privilege to be touched by so many people, many not mentioned here. I thank you all. And, finally, to everyone who picks up this book and takes the journey with me—using their business to make the world a better place—a big thank you. And good luck!

NOTES

Introduction

1. https://www.nasdaq.com/articles/5-best-performing-stocks-decade-2009-11-19.
2. https://www.forbes.com/sites/alejandrocremades/2019/07/02/the-chances-of-building-a-billion-dollar-business-are-00006-and-he-has-done-it-twice/?sh=70a5b9985588.
3. https://saylordotorg.github.io/text_the-sustainable-business-case-book/s13-03-sustainability-and-corporate-s.html.
4. 2021 IBM Institute for Business Value survey, https://www.ibm.com/downloads/cas/WLJ7LVP4.
5. https://www.moore-global.com/intelligence/articles/september-2022/%244trillion-esg-dividend.
6. https://www.gallup.com/workplace/236927/employee-engagement-drives-growth.aspx.
7. https://www.gallup.com/workplace/349484/state-of-the-global-workplace.aspx.
8. https://www.ibm.com/downloads/cas/WLJ7LVP4.
9. https://www.porternovelli.com/wp-content/uploads/2021/01/02_Porter-Novelli-Tracker-Wave-X-Employee-Perspectives-on-Responsible-Leadership-During-Crisis.pdf.
10. https://www.csrwire.com/press_releases/13665-green-mountain-coffee-roasters-tops-list-of-100-best-corporate-citizens-again.
11. https://case.edu/weatherhead/about/faculty-and-staff-directory/david-cooperrider.
12. https://www.forbes.com/sites/afdhelaziz/2020/03/07/the-power-of-purpose-the-business-case-for-purpose-all-the-data-you-were-looking-for-pt-2/?sh=6be8bc7b3cf7.
13. https://www.forbes.com/profile/robert-stiller/?sh=4b252be7491b.

14. https://www.nytimes.com/1984/08/04/business/capitalizing-on-halley -s-comet.html.
15. https://www.russellreynolds.com/en/insights/reports-surveys/global -ceo-turnover-index.
16. https://www.mckinsey.com/featured-insights/future-of-asia/four -steps-to-success-for-new-ceos.
17. https://medium.com/publishous/how-a-strategic-mistake-cost-home -depot-more-than-money-36a802d590ef.

Chapter 1

1. https://www.bls.gov/bdm/us_age_naics_00_table7.txt.
2. https://www.mckinsey.com/capabilities/strategy-and-corporate-finance/ our-insights/the-mindsets-and-practices-of-excellent-ceos.
3. https://hbr.org/2009/01/to-lead-create-a-shared-vision.
4. https://guayaki.com/blogs/the-gourd-circle/guayaki-co-founders -share-the-guayaki-journey-on-how-i-built-this.
5. https://www.forbes.com/sites/markmurphy/2018/04/15/neuroscience -explains-why-you-need-to-write-down-your-goals-if-you-actually -want-to-achieve-them/?sh=1a0751107905.
6. Shawn Achor, *Before Happiness: The 5 Hidden Keys to Achieving Success, Spreading Happiness, and Sustaining Positive Change*. (Crown Business, 2012), 9.
7. Dana Arakawa and Margaret Greenberg, "Optimistic Managers and Their Influence on Productivity and employee engagement in a Technology Organisation: Implications for Coaching Psychologists," *International Coaching Psychology Review*, Volume 2, no. 1 (March 2007): 78–89.
8. WhenDoOptimisticCEOsEnhanceFirmVal_preview.pdf.
9. https://www.pwc.com/gx/en/issues/c-suite-insights/ceo-survey-2023 .html.

Chapter 2

1. https://www.inc.com/tom-popomaronis/science-says-you-shouldnt -work-more-than-this-number-of-hours-a-day.html.
2. Reed Hastings and Erin Meyer, *No Rules Rules: Netflix and the Culture of Reinvention*. (Penguin Press, 2020.)
3. https://hbr.org/2021/10/how-companies-can-improve-employee -engagement-right-now; https://www.pwc.com/gx/en/services/ workforce/publications/nurture-agility-and-adaptability.html;

https://www.forbes.com/sites/steveforbes/2023/12/08/the-forbes
-2023-all-star-eateries-in-new-york/?sh=2283f153d993.5.

4. https://www.npr.org/2019/05/24/726755480/stacys-pita-chips-stacy
-madison.
5. https://vimeo.com/3461601.
6. https://www.benjerry.com/about-us/jobs#:~:text=Working%20at%20
Ben%20%26%20Jerry's&text=Ben%20%26%20Jerry's%20offers%20
a%20progressive,and%20frozen%20yogurt%20every%20day!.

Chapter 3

1. Mary Beth Grover, "Hippie Redux," *Forbes*, December 9, 1991, 326.
2. https://www.npr.org/2019/05/15/723670593/zappos-tony-hsieh.
3. https://www.deloittedigital.com/content/dam/deloittedigital/us/
documents/offerings/offering-20210614-future-of-sales.pdf.
4. https://ritzcarltonleadershipcenter.com/2022/04/06/i-am-proud-to
-be-ritz-carlton-a-look-at-our-service-values/.
5. https://www.forbes.com/sites/micahsolomon/2015/01/15/the
-amazing-true-story-of-the-hotel-that-saved-thomas-the-tank
-engine/?sh=6a50d688230e.
6. https://www.diageobaracademy.com/en_us/training/courses/.
7. https://www.linkedin.com/pulse/ibm-customer-success-what-does
-mean-frank-%C3%B8stergaard/.
8. https://info.thoughtindustries.com/hubfs/Downloadable%20Content/
IDC%20&%20Thought%20Industries%20-%20Investments%20
in%20Customer%20Education%20Lead%20to%20Growth%20
Program.pdf.
9. https://www.sfchronicle.com/sf/article/dreamforce-s-f-big-crowds
-openai-sam-altman-ai-18360762.php.
10. https://www.pleasantonweekly.com/news/2023/10/05/workday-rising
-conference-draws-largest-crowd-yet.
11. https://www.salesforce.com/blog/employee-satisfaction/.

Chapter 4

1. https://www.deloitte.com/global/en/issues/work/content/
genzmillennialsurvey.html.
2. https://www.goodnewsnetwork.org/top-100-corporations/.
3. https://www.greenbiz.com/article/toms-maine-where-csr-way-life.
4. https://www.forbes.com/sites/betsyatkins/2020/06/08/demystifying
-esg its-history--current-status/?sh=3a71229f2cdd.

5. https://www.moore-global.com/MediaLibsAndFiles/media/
MooreStephens2020/Documents/Moore_ESG_White-Paper_
FINAL.pdf.

6. https://www.ibm.com/downloads/cas/WLJ7LVP4.

7. https://www.csrwire.com/press_releases/13656-newman-s-own
-organics-green-mountain-coffee-roasters-launch-cause-related
-organic-fair-trade-certified-coffees.

8. https://www.csrwire.com/press_releases/13661-green-mountain
-coffee-roasters-tops-business-ethics-list-of-100-best-corporate
-citizens.

9. https://www.youtube.com/watch?v=e1TPIPZKdXo.

10. https://www.wholeplanetfoundation.org/get-involved/whole-foods
-market-team-member-volunteer-program/.

11. https://www.fool.com/investing/general/2013/10/14/can-green
-mountain-coffee-bounce-back.aspx.

12. https://www.tomsofmaine.com/news/toms-of-maine-gives-500000
-to-inspirational-nonprofits#:~:text=Since%20it%20was%20founded
%20in,off%20to%20volunteer%20every%20year.

13. https://theconversation.com/us-charitable-donations-fell-to-499
-billion-in-2022-as-stocks-slumped-and-inflation-surged-207688#:~
:text=The%20Giving%20USA%20data%20shows,less%20money%20
to%20give%20away.

14. https://www.keurigdrpepper.com/content/dam/keurig-brand-sites/
kdp/files/GMCRSustainabilityReport_2012.pdf.

15. https://web.archive.org/web/20220207090608/https://www.
keurigdrpepper.com/content/dam/keurig-brand-sites/kdp/files/
KeurigSustainabilityReport_2013.pdf.

16. https://www.forbes.com/sites/afdhelaziz/2020/03/07/the-power-of
-purpose-the-business-case-for-purpose-all-the-data-you-were
-looking-for-pt-2/?sh=6be8bc7b3cf7.

17. https://www.salesforce.org/about/pledge/; https://stakeholder
impactreport.salesforce.com/social/supporting-our-communities#:~
:text=In%20FY23%2C%20Salesforce%20reached%20over,and%20
communities%20around%20the%20world.

18. https://communications.fidelity.com/pdf/wg-accp-research-report.pdf.

19. https://www.progressive.com/careers/life/good-in-our-communities/.

20. https://doublethedonation.com/matching-gifts/netflix.

21. https://news.microsoft.com/source/features/work-life/employee
-giving/.

22. David L. Cooperrider and Ronald E. Fry, "Mirror Flourishing and the Positive Psychology of Sustainability," *Journal of Corporate Citizenship*, 46 (June 2012), 3–12.

Chapter 5

1. Stephen R. Covey, *The 7 Habits of Highly Effective People* (Simon & Schuster, 1989), 287.
2. https://vermontbiz.com/news/2008/october/15/green-mountain-coffee-roasters-inc-climbs-forbes-200-best-small-companies.
3. https://www.apa.org/pubs/reports/work-in-america/2023-workplace-health-well-being#:~:text=The%20results%20of%20APA's%202023, emotional%20and%20psychological%20well%2Dbeing.
4. https://www.microsoft.com/en-gb/industry/blog/cross-industry/2019/10/01/introduce-learn-it-all-culture/.
5. https://www.shrm.org/topics-tools/research/2022-2023-shrm-state-workplace.
6. https://initiatives.weforum.org/reskilling-revolution/home.
7. https://www.apa.org/pubs/reports/work-in-america/2023-workplace-health-well-being.
8. Amazon_Upskilling_Report.pdf at https://www.gallup.com/analytics/506696/amazon-research-hub.aspx#ite-506726.
9. https://sloanreview.mit.edu/article/toxic-culture-is-driving-the-great-resignation/.
10. https://www.nceo.org/article/key-studies-employee-ownership-and-corporate-performance.
11. https://www.ownershipeconomy.org/research/.
12. https://cleo.rutgers.edu/wp-content/uploads/2020/11/EOF-REPORT-EMPLOYEE-OWNED-FIRMS-IN-THE-COVID-19-PANDEMIC.pdf.
13. https://forum.gettingthingsdone.com/threads/david-allen-in-vermont-3-8-2004.756/.
14. https://www.gallup.com/394424/indicator-employee-wellbeing.aspx16.
15. https://www.apa.org/pubs/reports/work-in-america/2023-workplace-health-well-being#:~:text=The%20results%20of%20APA's%20 2023,emotional%20and%20psychological%20well%2Dbeing.
16. https://www.gallup.com/394424/indicator-employee-wellbeing.aspx.
17. https://mag.toyota.co.uk/kaizen-toyota-production-system/.
18. https://hbr.org/2022/12/research-when-mindfulness-does-and-doesnt-help-at-work.

19. https://www.emerald.com/insight/content/doi/10.1108/EJTD-09
-2019-0156/full/html; https://www.ncbi.nlm.nih.gov/pmc/articles/
PMC4846034/; https://www.ncbi.nlm.nih.gov/pmc/articles/
PMC6088366/.
20. https://gumc.georgetown.edu/news-release/mindfulness-based
-stress-reduction-is-as-effective-as-an-antidepressant-drug-for
-treating-anxiety-disorders/#:~:text=WASHINGTON%20
(November%209%2C%202022),led%20by%20researchers%20at%20
Georgetown.
21. https://www.microsoft.com/en-us/worklab/work-trend-index/great
-expectations-making-hybrid-work-work.
22. https://www.gallup.com/workplace/349484/state-of-the-global
-workplace.aspx.
23. https://cecp.co/home/resources/giving-in-numbers/.
24. https://doublethedonation.com/matching-gifts/aetn.
25. https://workdaybenefits.com/ca/more-to-love/giving-back#:~:text=
Team%20volunteer%20grants,can%20request%20in%20a%20year!.
26. https://www.ifebp.org/store/employee-benefits-survey/Pages/default
.aspx.
27. https://www.weforum.org/agenda/2022/12/hybrid-working-remote
-work-office-senior-leaders/.

Chapter 6

1. Luisa Kroll, "Java Man," *Forbes*, October 29, 2001, 142.
2. Jacqueline Stavros, Lindsey N. Godwin, and David L. Cooperrider, "Appreciative Inquiry: Organization Development and the Strengths Revolution," in *Practicing Organization Development: Leading Transformation and Change*, eds. William Rothwell, Jacqueline Stavros, and Roland Sullivan (John Wiley and Sons, 2016), 96-116.
3. David L. Coopperrider and D. Whitney, "A Positive Revolution in Change," in *Appreciative Inquiry: An Emerging Direction for Organization Development*, eds. Cooperrider, Sorenson, Whitney, and Yeager (Stipes Publishing, 2001), 9-29.
4. https://www.apa.org/topics/healthy-workplaces/mental-health/listen
-employee-needs.
5. https://www.mckinsey.com/capabilities/people-and-organizational
-performance/our-insights/raising-the-resilience-of-your-organization.
6. David Allen, *Ready for Anything: 52 Productivity Principles for Getting Things Done* (Penguin Books, 2004), 106.

7. https://www.psychologicalscience.org/news/minds-business/how-to
-become-the-smartest-group-in-the-room.html.

Chapter 7

1. Bain & Company, M&A Report 2024. Download from: https://www
.bain.com/insights/topics/m-and-a-report/.
2. https://hbr.org/2011/03/the-big-idea-the-new-ma-playbook.
3. https://www.mckinsey.com/capabilities/people-and-organizational
-performance/our-insights/organizational-culture-in-mergers
-addressing-the-unseen-forces.
4. https://www.bizjournals.com/boston/stories/2006/05/01/daily33.html.
5. https://hbr.org/2018/10/one-reason-mergers-fail-the-two-cultures
-arent-compatible.
6. https://www.theguardian.com/business/2018/oct/01/whole-foods
-amazon-union-organization-grocery-chain.
7. https://www.cnbc.com/2018/09/06/whole-foods-employees-want-to
-unionize-under-amazon-ownership.html.
8. https://www.bloomberg.com/news/articles/2022-08-31/amazon-s
-whole-foods-deal-has-delivered-mixed-results.
9. https://www.theguardian.com/us-news/2020/jan/05/berkeley
-california-disposable-cup-law.
10. https://nestle-nespresso.com/our-history.

Chapter 8

1. Foreword by Padraig Harrington, in Bob Rotella, *Make Your Next
Shot Your Best Shot: The Secret to Playing Great Golf* (Simon &Schuster,
2021).
2. https://www.shrm.org/executive/resources/people-strategy-journal/
fall2021/pages/art-of-leaving-ciampa.aspx.
3. https://hbr.org/2016/12/after-the-handshake.
4. https://www.strategyand.pwc.com/gx/en/insights/ceo-success.html#
Strategymadereal.
5. https://www.marketwatch.com/story/nardellis-arrogance-led-to
-downfall-analysts; https://www.wired.com/2013/12/home-depot
-reinvents-buckets/.
6. https://hbr.org/2023/02/beware-the-transition-from-an-iconic-ceo.
7. Ibid.
8. https://www.gsb.stanford.edu/sites/default/files/publication/pdfs/cgri
-closer-look-95-firing-hiring-ceo.pdf; https://www.gsb.stanford.edu/

sites/default/files/publication-pdf/cgri-closer-look-45-handpicked
-ceo-successor.pdf.

9. https://www.strategy-business.com/article/Succeeding-the-long
-serving-legend-in-the-corner-office.

10. Ibid.

11. https://smallbiztrends.com/2015/05/keurig-ceo-regret-mistake
-keurig-20.html.

12. https://www.benjerry.com/about-us?through-the-decades=tab-2000s.

13. https://www.nytimes.com/2022/09/14/climate/patagonia-climate
-philanthropy-chouinard.html.

14. https://www.patagoniaworks.com/press/2022/9/14/patagonias-next
-chapter-earth-is-now-our-only-shareholder.

15. https://hbr.org/2015/01/where-boards-fall-short.

16. Luisa Kroll, "Java Man Is Newest Billionaire," *Forbes*, March 6, 2011,
https://www.forbes.com/sites/luisakroll/2011/03/16/java-man-is
-newest-billionaire/?sh=6623ff3f51e6.

17. https://www.businessinsider.com/gaap-uccino-the-story-of-keurigs
-coffee-dominance-2011-10; https://www.forbes.com/sites/
afontevecchia/2012/05/08/the-precipitous-decline-of-green
-mountain-coffees-founders-fortune/?sh=6c88699267ef.

Chapter 9

1. https://www.literacymidsouth.org/news/the-relationship-between
-incarceration-and-low-literacy#:~:text=Politicians%20and%20
journalists%20often%20claim,our%20country's%20exploding%20
incarceration%20rates.

2. https://www.ojp.gov/ncjrs/virtual-library/abstracts/prison-literacy
-connection.

3. https://www.fairtradecertified.org/about-us/board-of-directors/.

4. https://www.bonehealthandosteoporosis.org/wp-content/uploads/
Osteoporosis-Fast-Facts-2.pdf.

5. https://heckmanequation.org/resource/the-heckman-curve.

6. https://letsgrowkids.org/client_media/files/LGK_2022ImpactReport_
OUT_Digital-SinglePg%20Final.pdf.

7. A. H. Maslow (1943). "A Theory of Human Motivation," *Psychological Review*, 50(4): 370–396. https://doi.org/10.1037/h005434.6.

8. https://positivepsychology.com/self-transcendence/#:~:text=According
%20to%20Maslow%2C%20self%2Dtranscendence,awareness%20
(Messerly%2C%202017).

INDEX

ABOUT THE AUTHOR

Bob Stiller is an American entrepreneur who cofounded E-Z Wider in 1971 and then Green Mountain Coffee Roasters (GMCR) in 1981 serving as its chief executive officer and president from 1981 to 2007. He was named *Forbes'* first "Entrepreneur of the Year" in 2001 and one of *Investor's Business Daily*'s "Top 10 leaders and successful CEOs" for transforming the humble Vermont coffee roaster into one of the most financially successful companies of the past 25 years. He built GMCR into a multibillion-dollar coffee empire by embracing the idea that businesses can make the world a better place when they focus on social responsibility, prioritize employee and stakeholder engagement, and provide a great place to work. Mr. Stiller was instrumental in the Fair Trade coffee movement and under his direction, GMCR became the largest supplier of Fair Trade coffee in the world. He continues to model a commitment to corporate responsibility and public service through the Stiller Family Foundation that focuses on helping people help themselves. The Stiller Family Foundation received the 2013 Outstanding Foundation Award from the Association of Fundraising Professionals.